bliss
happens

bliss

happens

the six-week plan to a happier,
prettier, thinner, and richer life

kym douglas

Published in Los Angeles, California, by Bird Street Books, Inc.

ISBN: 978-0-9854627-1-0

Cover Design: Hagop Kalaidjian
Interior Design: Maureen Forys, Happenstance Type-O-Rama

Acknowledgments

How do you write a book about Bliss without surrounding yourself with Blissful people? You don't! So, I'd like to thank all the people in my life who have brought me Bliss and helped me share it with the world. Thank you to my collaborator, producer, and now sister, Lisa Clark, for your contributions to this book and for your friendship. And to Scott Waterbury with Bird Street Books, thank you for your involvement in this Blissful project. Scott, your true strength comes from your depth of character and quality of soul. You're all heart, and you have such a wonderful way with everyone who crosses your path. To Chelsea Wright, for all the ways you've been instrumental in researching and nurturing this book. You are a beauty, inside and out. And to Hagop Kalaidjian, for the many hats you wear and roles you have played in the creation and promotion of this book and brand. Ophelia Soumekh, my business partner and cherished friend: Thank you for being by my side and supporting me every day since the day we met. And I certainly can't leave out the amazing talents at BWR Public Relations. Paul Baker and Larry Winokur, thank you for the many years of support you've given me and Jerry. You and your team are simply brilliant and deserve all the success, acclaim, and Bliss you have achieved worldwide. Jay McGraw, the man at the helm, this book could never have come to life without your vision, your input, and your willingness. You are a maverick in the best sense of the word, and it is a pure delight working with you. And thank you, Jeff Hudson, for believing in me and seeing the big picture. So much has come together because of your foresight, and I'm grateful. And to my angel, Matt Wright, who changed my life. All of this is because of you! Of course, to the three executive producers of *The Ellen Degeneres Show*: Andy Lassner, Mary Connelly, and Ed Glavin—thank you for your unwavering support and faith in me. Finally, thank you, Ellen DeGeneres, for giving me a platform to spread happiness, laughter, kindness, and, in a word, Bliss...to the world!

Dedication

This book is dedicated to the two people who have brought more bliss to my life than I ever thought possible: my husband, Jerry, who walked into my life 28 years ago and introduced me to a level of love and happiness that I had only dreamed about, and our son, Hunter William. Hunter, from the moment you were born, you have brought me pure and utter bliss!

Contents

Introduction

What is *Bliss* to you? What would make you truly happy? It's a question we don't often ask ourselves because most of the time we are too busy struggling through our "have tos" instead of discovering our "want tos." I am challenging you to start thinking about it because you have to define it in order to work toward it. Does Bliss mean having a lot of money, fame, or unforgettable beauty? Do you look at celebrities and think they must have it "all?" I have to tell you: I've met plenty of people in my life who have all of that and more, yet they still don't have Bliss. Bliss is not about chasing fame, fortune, or anything else fleeting. Let me explain.

You've heard people call the young starlets who land on the cover of magazines the newest "it" girls. Well, I think the "it factor" that all the Hollywood agents, talent scouts, and panels of judges on those singing competition shows are looking for is actually the "Bliss Factor." There's a certain look in her eyes, a calm confidence in the way she carries herself, a conviction she projects when she speaks, and an aura that surrounds someone when she has "it." She leaves an imprint behind, something you can't easily forget.

You can't touch it, but you sure can feel it. The truth is you don't need to have the voice of a songbird or the looks of a model to have the Bliss Factor. I believe everyone has the capacity for it—you just have to find it and then learn how to raise its volume.

I want you to live the life you think all those A-list celebs are living. How can you have that life? It has a lot to do with making the absolute most of what you have: your body, your face, your home, your family, your finances, and more. When it all comes together, you're left feeling complete and utter Bliss. Not all of the time—but you can have Bliss in your life most of the time if you stick to my formula: Do more with less. I'm going to show you how to improve upon so many areas of your stressed-out life while simplifying things. For instance, rather than spending money on expensive spa products and skin treatments, I'll show you how you can use some of the ingredients you're already putting in your breakfast to anti-age your skin. But this book is about so much more than slathering some blueberries on your face! I'll also enlighten you with fun, informative, and simple ways to take your body, home, energy level, man, and many other aspects of your life to a whole new level of amazing. Some of your Bliss will come from following my plans for looking and feeling your best. And some of it will have to come from within. (I'll hold your hand for that part, too!)

Whether you're already in a pretty good place and just want to live, look, and feel even better or you're in a temporary funk or maybe your life has you feeling like Bridget Jones on her worst day over and over again, allow me to be your knight in shining body shapers! *Bliss Happens* is a simple, step-by-step guide that'll help you look gorgeous, feel fantastic, and fall desperately in love with your life. And don't worry; I've done all the thinking and research for you, so all you have to do is put it into action. Of course, there will still be challenges, and life will still throw you curve balls. But I'm here to help you gain confidence, look in the mirror and like what you see, and feel healthier physically, emotionally, and even in terms of your living space and overall environment. Ultimately, you will feel better about yourself and your life without breaking the bank or your back.

We can all agree that life isn't perfect. I checked, and there was no blowout sale on "perfect lives" at Target today. Seriously, though, ask yourself this: Would you really want life to be "perfect?" I think that when things go wrong, we get the opportunity to learn the most about ourselves and our incredible ability to rise to the occasion. Aren't the bumps in the road what make the trip exciting? Even if someone offered me a "perfect life" on a silver platter, I'd choose the one I have any day of the week. That's because my imperfect life is Blissful—and yours can be, too.

How My Bliss Niche Was Born

You might be wondering who I think I am to tell you how to find your Bliss. Let me introduce myself. I'm Kym Douglas, author, beauty and lifestyle expert, TV host, comedienne, red carpet reporter, mom, wife, and plate-spinner extraordinaire. (The plate spinning is a metaphor. Heaven forbid someone make me do that for real! I'm just saying I've gotten pretty darn good at multitasking.)

If you follow the trail of my career, your journey will start in the stall of a public restroom! Yep, I'm serious. I was working at E! Entertainment News in Hollywood, and they had a new program called *The Gossip Show*. They asked me to be one of the reporters for that show. I had come from a hard-news anchor background in Michigan, so I was over the moon and ready to start on the Hollywood beat. There was only one tiny problem. Not to sound like a goody-two shoes, but I didn't want to report gossip... at least, not the negative kind. Obviously, I know that everyone loves hearing about which celebrity is having an affair with her director, who's breaking the law, and other juicy tidbits about their lives, but that just isn't my passion. I'd much rather find out the insider secrets the stars are using to keep their skin glowing, their hair crazy shiny, and their bodies super fit. So, the pressure was on. My job was on the line. Report on the celebs' "dirt" (think pre-TMZ) or I was O-U-T. What's a girl to do?

My first interview out of the gate was with an A-list actress starring in a hit cable series. I had a decision to make. Was I going to pounce and see what kind of dirt I could get on this stunning celebrity so I could keep my job? Or was I going to just ask the questions that I knew regular women like me really wanted to know? I started off with my usual hard-hitting investigative reporting line of questioning: "What are your beauty secrets, if you don't mind me asking?" Lo and behold, I had just opened a Pandora's Box of Beauty. We talked about how, regardless of the wealth Hollywood stars had, they still appreciate a fantastic sale or great ideas for saving money, just like the rest of us. My favorite tip we discussed was using toilet seat covers (from a public restroom!) to blot an oily T-zone. Why buy blotting papers when a quick stop in the stall has all we need? *Beyond*!

When my bosses saw it, they were thrilled, and my niche was born. Celebs would get to share their tricks of the trade that keep them looking red-carpet gorgeous, and I would get to report their insider beauty tips to women (and men!) everywhere. What's not to love? So, from my adolescent pipe dream to my post-college hard-news anchoring outside of Detroit to Hollywood DIY beauty (with a pinch of humor and fun), my little niche has grown and evolved. Now, I'm excited to go a little deeper with you and share all the secrets I've learned over the years, both from the rich and famous and from my own experiences, for how to truly have a Blissful life.

Are You Your Own Bliss Frenemy?

Every woman has had a frenemy at some point. You know, that person who pretends to be your friend, but she's actually insanely jealous of you and finds subtle (or overt!) ways to sabotage you and your happiness. She tries to keep you as far from your Bliss as humanly possible. Maybe you still haven't forgiven your frenemy from grade school who stole your boyfriend, but I have news for you—it's possible that the worst frenemy you've ever had is you. She's with you everywhere you go, and man, can she be relentless. I bet there have been times when you've told yourself you're not bright enough, pretty enough, witty enough, or charming enough to have your dreams come true. You think, "I'm too fat for that guy to notice me" or "I'm not smart enough to do that job" or, simply, "I can't do it." Those four little words can hold so much power if you let them. In fact, I almost let those four words sabotage my entire career.

Picture it: A popular bookstore in West Hollywood on a cold, rainy night. (All good stories begin on a rainy night, don't they?) It was the final stop on my book tour for *The Black Book of Hollywood Beauty Secrets*. Maybe the 1 inch of rain was to blame for the rather low attendance at the signing (ten people total, two of whom were my husband, Jerry, and our son, Hunter), or maybe the room was empty because I'd already bribed all my friends and acquaintances to go to previous signings so the jig was up. But I didn't let the poor turnout phase me. I had an audience, and it didn't matter how big or small it was. I pulled out all the stops, showing off the zaniest of the beauty tips from my book. There I was, a one-woman band, smearing glue on my nose as a blackhead remover and using toilet seat covers to blot oil on my face, when suddenly I noticed my husband, Jerry, yakking it up in the front row with one of my loyal friends who came out to support me.

I glared at Jerry from the podium through squinted eyes, trying to get him to pipe down, but he just kept chatting away! Satisfied with the chuckles from audience members, I wrapped up the demo and started to pack up, refusing to even make eye contact with Jerry at this point. I was fuming mad! How could he have the nerve to sit in the front row, not pay one ounce of attention to me, and disrupt my presentation? I thanked everyone for coming, signed a couple books, and got ready to leave. When Jerry finally told me what had been so important that he couldn't stop talking through my entire spiel, my jaw dropped to the floor. See, my friend he'd been chatting with was a producer at *The Ellen DeGeneres Show*. My husband had been sitting there pitching the idea of me (yes, *me*!) going on *Ellen* and sharing my beauty secrets with her and the world. He wouldn't take no for an answer—he just kept selling him on how funny I'd be with Ellen and that she would love my whole routine. I could've died. What if my friend thought I was the one who put Jerry up to this? Honestly, I'd never once thought about going on *Ellen*; it never would have crossed my mind! And now suddenly my husband was pushing the idea on my friend without even consulting me. I was mortified.

Five days passed, and I was too embarrassed to call my friend, so when his number showed up on my caller ID, I wasn't sure what I was going to say. I didn't have to worry about it for long because the first words out of his mouth were, "Ellen is hosting the Academy Awards, and I pitched the idea of you coming on the show to share your Hollywood beauty secrets to get her ready for the red carpet. The executive producers loved it. You're coming on the show next week!" Confident and calm as could be, I replied, "Great! I'll be there!" I hung up the phone and promptly ran back to my bed and crawled under the covers. My inner frenemy had come out to play, and she didn't play fair. My mind raced: I wasn't ready, this was too big, I'm not funny, Ellen won't like me, the audience won't laugh, I'll freeze up, I'll never work again in television, I will ruin my career. I sank further into my frenemy funk even as friends and family called to congratulate me and *ooh* and *aah* over this huge opportunity (since Jerry had, of course, told them about it). I came to the final conclusion and my four little words, "I can't do it."

To really grasp the breadth of this next part, I should share with you that I've always had a nervous stomach—not the girly kind of nervous stomach where you get butterflies and perhaps a slight queasiness. Oh, nooo. My nervous stomach is the kind that makes you throw up—nonstop—for hours on end. That kind of nervous stomach. And so, when the first wave of nausea hit the day before the *Ellen* show was taping, I knew I was in trouble.

I couldn't leave the bathroom for eight hours straight, and I knew it was impossible for me to appear on television the next morning. My "I can't do it" motto had won. And sadly, it wasn't even that tough of a fight. With that croaky puke voice, I called and tearfully told my friend I couldn't do the segment, already feeling some relief as the words left my dry, cracked lips. But the nausea came back in a tidal wave when he wouldn't take no for an answer. "It's too late, Kym. We can't get anyone else now. You have to show up." With a dial tone in my ear and mere hours until cameras started rolling, I felt nothing but sheer terror.

My reaction made absolutely no sense—was I actually trying to destroy my future and my career? This was what I'd always wanted, wasn't it? All obstacles had been cleared, so why was I now barfing myself into oblivion? A stroke of genius (or delirium) hit me, and I called a friend who knew a doctor who made house calls. An hour later, the doctor showed up at my door to find my weak, disheveled, still-vomiting self on the bathroom floor. She took mercy on me and gave me a miraculous pill that caused the vomiting to cease and desist. I didn't know how long it would last, but I was grateful for the breather anyway.

When I arrived at the *Ellen* studio in Burbank the next morning, the producers took one look at me and probably thought *their* TV careers were over! I looked like the furthest thing from an expert on beauty and Hollywood glamour, unless you consider "Rehab Chic" to be a popular look. I was white as a sheet, hunched over, and puffy-eyed. Still, I was determined not to let my fear of failure get the best of me. I knew deep inside I could do it. (Cue the *Rocky* music.)

The remarkable hair, makeup, and wardrobe teams at *Ellen* tapped into some kind of TV magic and managed to curl, fluff, cinch, and paint me back to looking human. (I admit, even TV-ready.) My stomach continued its reprieve, though I remember feeling parched because I'd denied myself even the tiniest sip of water for fear of a projectile vomit moment all over Ellen. I was waiting anxiously in the greenroom as the seconds ticked by on the clock. And then, I heard Ellen's warm and funny voice shout, "Welcome, Kym Douglas!" as the studio audience clapped.

The second I walked out on that stage, all my nerves just melted away, and I felt tingly—I was home. There were no voices inside my head putting myself down, no external distractions, just 100 percent confidence in the message I had and where I was conveying it, with millions of people watching. It was like magic—with no effort at all, Ellen and I cracked up through the entire segment, and the audience seemed to love it. Even the stuff I didn't think would get nary a smile brought down the house. A wave of something washed over me. What was that something? It was Bliss. And six years later, the producers tell me I've been on Ellen's show more than any other guest or expert.

Appearing on *Ellen* is certainly Blissful for me because I love sharing all of my beauty and lifestyle secrets with others. But that isn't my only source of Bliss. I work at my Bliss every single day, and it comes from so many outlets. My intent is for you to realize that no matter what's holding you back—your inner frenemy or anything else—now is the time to define and pursue your Bliss. I'm here to help you every step of the way.

Part 1

The Bliss Basics

You're probably thinking, "Like the title of this book, make Bliss happen for me!" We're getting there, I promise. Bliss can happen for anyone, but it takes work, so first we need to lay the foundation. This isn't the kind of plan where you can just skip right to the page that says what to do on Day 1 and hope you'll get results. This requires a little bit of soul searching and some personal reinvention.

Not to break it down into too simplistic of an analogy, but when you go on a diet to lose weight, you realize that it's going to take some work on your part. The fat doesn't magically melt off your body just because you bought a diet book and stopped going to the drive-thru (though those are commendable first steps). There are other steps you have to take—such as throwing away junk foods, buying healthy foods, actually eating those healthy foods, counting calories, exercising, and so on. Soon, the pounds begin to vanish, thanks to the effort you are putting in. Well, the same is true when you're on a mission to increase your Bliss: There are multiple steps involved, and you have to be prepared.

The following chapter will help you gauge your current level of Bliss. Yep, just like you know how much you weigh, there's a scale that will reveal your Bliss Factor. You'll be able to clearly define just how happy you are with the state of affairs in your life so you can start making serious inroads to a whole new level of happiness in all the right places. It will also spell out what Bliss means (literally—I made it into an acronym, which I knew you would love) and how the Bliss Plan at the end of this book will help you find it in your own life.

Chapter 2, "Inner Bliss," will give you some general dos and don'ts to follow in order to boost your Bliss, which is basically like building your foundation. Remember what happens to houses built on the sand—they fall apart and sink right into the ocean! I don't want your Bliss falling apart and drowning, so let's build on some serious bedrock. Sound good? I'm so excited to get you started. Let's go!

Chapter 1

How Blissful Are You?

What is Bliss? There's the dictionary definition of "supreme happiness or utter joy"—no wonder we all want it! But I also look at the word *Bliss* as an acronym. For our purposes, *Bliss* now stands for Beauty, Living, Inexpensive, Simplicity, and Solutions. Each one is a vital component in my overall Bliss Plan.

BLISS

Beauty: Every morning before you leave the house, I want you to look and feel like you just stepped off the red carpet. I'm talking about the part where you love what you see in the mirror so much that you almost can't stop looking. Your skin is glowing, your eyes are dazzling, your body is firm, your teeth are white, and even your posture screams "I'm Blissful!" I'll show you how you can achieve this type of beauty, working both from the inside out and from the outside in.

Living: Yes, you're already living. But follow this plan, and you'll experience a different kind of living as you look forward to every day, wake up energized, and feel at peace and confident. It's a totally different experience when you feel like you're doing what you want to be doing and everyone around you starts responding differently to you because you're giving off positive energy. I know your lifestyle isn't entirely within your control, but so many factors of it are, and it's our job to maximize those so you can truly enjoy every day.

Inexpensive: Living Blissfully is not about making millions; it's about making the most of what you do have. How can you feel Bliss if you're throwing all your precious pennies toward pricey products that may or may not actually make you more beautiful or make your life more organized? I will show you how you can accomplish all of it on a shoestring budget. There are so many ways I help you stretch your dollar further than ever. I love to do more with less, and I can't wait to share with you how!

Simplicity: I know it's hard to imagine a simple life when you have competing commitments, young children, a to-do list you can't even find, and friends you don't have time to see. That's where simplicity comes into play. I'm giving you the tools you need to get the kind of life you've dreamed about living—one that lets you actually stop and smell the roses and still keep all the trains running on time in your household, at work, anywhere. You truly can have it all *and* enjoy it.

Solutions: Thank goodness there are two s's in *Bliss* because where would we be without the solutions? This book is overflowing with simple, inexpensive solutions designed to help you feel happier by simplifying and amplifying your life. I promise you're going to feel silly when you're using some of my techniques, but laughing at yourself is a huge component of Bliss, so it's all part of the plan!

What's Your Bliss Factor?

We measure our weight in pounds and temperature in degrees, but how do you measure Bliss? It's not quite as simple, but you measure what I call your Bliss Factor by using a Bliss Scale. You should know, at any given moment, just how happy you really are with the state of affairs in your life because if you know it, you can improve it. I want you to have a goal for just how Blissful you want to be! Dream big, dolls!

Take the following quiz, and find your score on the Bliss Scale.

Your current Bliss Factor is your "before" number, so be sure to write it down. After you complete my plan, your "after" Bliss Factor is going to amaze you.

The Bliss Quiz

WHAT YOU DO

For each statement, choose the response that you agree with the most. Don't over-think each one—go with your gut!

1. I set realistic goals for myself, and I know what it takes to reach them.

    A. Heck yes, sistah!

    B. Yep, I kinda agree with that.

    C. Whatevs.

    D. Not so much.

    E. No way! Are you crazy, lady?

2. I'm grateful for my life and all of its gifts. I don't feel like I'm lacking anything or envious of what others have.

   A. Heck yes, sistah!

   B. Yep, I kinda agree with that.

   C. Whatevs.

   D. Not so much.

   E. No way! Are you crazy, lady?

3. I'm tuned into my inner voice, and I know what I want out of life.

   A. Heck yes, sistah!

   B. Yep, I kinda agree with that.

   C. Whatevs.

   D. Not so much.

   E. No way! Are you crazy, lady?

4. I have a solid relationship with myself—I refrain from dishing out insults to myself (even when I've gained a couple pounds), and my self-esteem is intact.

   A. Heck yes, sistah!

   B. Yep, I kinda agree with that.

   C. Whatevs.

   D. Not so much.

   E. No way! Are you crazy, lady?

5. I know I should put myself first sometimes because the kids, pets, or anyone else who depends on me will be better off for it.

   A. Heck yes, sistah!

   B. Yep, I kinda agree with that.

   C. Whatevs.

   D. Not so much.

   E. No way! Are you crazy, lady?

6. My skin looks fabulous, I rarely have breakouts, and I have a great regime to keep the wrinkles and age spots at bay.

    A. Heck yes, sistah!

    B. Yep, I kinda agree with that.

    C. Whatevs.

    D. Not so much.

    E. No way! Are you crazy, lady?

7. I smile proudly because my teeth are dazzling and my lips are plump, soft, and silky.

    A. Heck yes, sistah!

    B. Yep, I kinda agree with that.

    C. Whatevs.

    D. Not so much.

    E. No way! Are you crazy, lady?

8. My hair is shiny, healthy, voluminous, and soft. I could practically be in a shampoo commercial!

    A. Heck yes, sistah!

    B. Yep, I kinda agree with that.

    C. Whatevs.

    D. Not so much.

    E. No way! Are you crazy, lady?

9. I'm so pleased with the current state of my fingernails and toe-nails that I purposely talk with my hands and wish I could wear open-toe shoes year-round.

    A. Heck yes, sistah!

    B. Yep, I kinda agree with that.

    C. Whatevs.

    D. Not so much.

    E. No way! Are you crazy, lady?

10. My eyes are rarely, if ever, puffy or have black circles underneath them.

    A. Heck yes, sistah!

    B. Yep, I kinda agree with that.

    C. Whatevs.

    D. Not so much.

    E. No way! Are you crazy, lady?

11. When I look around the spaces in which I primarily live and work, I see organization and, décor that makes me smile, and I'm proud to show off these rooms to friends and family (yes, even my closet).

    A. Heck yes, sistah!

    B. Yep, I kinda agree with that.

    C. Whatevs.

    D. Not so much.

    E. No way! Are you crazy, lady?

12. I practically bounce out of bed when the alarm goes off (and I hardly need an alarm most days), I have great energy throughout the day (even in the afternoon), and I'm rarely tired.

    A. Heck yes, sistah!

    B. Yep, I kinda agree with that.

    C. Whatevs.

    D. Not so much.

    E. No way! Are you crazy, lady?

13. I give off a happy, calm, confident energy most of the time.

    A. Heck yes, sistah!

    B. Yep, I kinda agree with that.

    C. Whatevs.

    D. Not so much.

    E. No way! Are you crazy, lady?

14. I'm happy with how my body looks (in clothes and in the buff), and I'm really good about choosing the right foods and exercises to keep it that way.

    A. Heck yes, sistah!

    B. Yep, I kinda agree with that.

    C. Whatevs.

    D. Not so much.

    E. No way! Are you crazy, lady?

15. My entire household (including kids, pets, and anyone else living under my roof) runs in better harmony than a performance on *Glee*.

    A. Heck yes, sistah!

    B. Yep, I kinda agree with that.

    C. Whatevs.

    D. Not so much.

    E. No way! Are you crazy, lady?

Here is your point breakdown:

A answers = 4 points

B answers = 3 points

C answers = 2 points

D answers = 1 point

E answers = 0 points

Add up your total number of points, and record your current Bliss Factor here.

My Current Bliss Factor Is: _____

So, what the heck does that number mean? Here's a scale to help you get a grasp of the current state of your Bliss. Don't be discouraged by your number because the goal is to boost your Bliss over the next six weeks by at least ten points...or more! Or, better yet, go for a perfect 60!

The Bliss Scale

51-60: Bliss is practically my middle name. My house makes me feel like I just stepped into the pages of *Elle Décor*, I love who I see staring back at me in the mirror, I appreciate all my little victories, and life is utterly Blissful. (I'd love for you to keep reading and inspire someone else with Bliss, but heck, you could put the book down now!)

41-50: I'm whistling a happy tune a lot of the time, and I'm pretty confident with myself. I understand what makes me Blissful, but I do spend more time than I should feeling like something is missing. I should make my happiness a little more of a priority.

31-40: I don't hate my appearance, but I could like it more. My house isn't total chaos, but it doesn't exactly inspire Bliss (especially when I open the closet door).

21-30: I don't consider myself beautiful, organized, or at peace, but I think I could be, if I just knew how. I'm aware of the fact that I should do more for myself, and I'm envious of women who seem to have it all together. Are they on something?

11-20: I'm presentable...some of the time. My household is borderline pandemonium. I'm usually frazzled, but I'm not quite ready to be declared a "state of emergency."

1-10: I wouldn't know happiness if it slapped me silly. I can't really remember the last time I smiled without forcing it. I detest mirrors, and it takes me an hour to find my keys every morning. I'm a hot mess.

0: I'm going through the motions of life in a zombielike way. I get by, but I feel like I'm hanging by a thread a lot of the time. The only thing I feel like I have going for me is that I'm breathing. I am breathing, right?

How to Implement the Bliss Plan

The Bliss Plan is a simple, six-week routine broken into three parts. There's a one-week Beauty Bliss Routine, a one-week Living Bliss Plan, and a thirty-day overall Bliss Plan. The first two weeks set you up for success during the one-month plan. I am all about simplicity, so there's nothing complicated about this plan. Promise!

The purpose of your one-week Beauty Bliss Plan is to set you sailing on the course for Bliss. During that week, I'll help you identify and get rid of the "stuff" in your life that's stealing your happiness and begin to raise the volume on the things that boost your Bliss. It focuses on your inner Bliss and outer beauty because they're a lot more connected than you might realize, and it prepares your body and mind for the next steps. I think you'll be amazed by what you can accomplish in just seven days with tasks that you can easily incorporate into your everyday schedule. You'll even begin feeling and seeing changes right away.

After those seven glorious days, you'll begin the one-week Living Bliss Plan, which you can also easily integrate into your busy lifestyle. This seven-day Bliss pregame, if you will, focuses on a literal cleanout of your home and schedule, setting you up for a smooth-running household and lifestyle.

Next, you'll start my 30-day overall Bliss Plan, a comprehensive daily strategy that is sure to majorly upgrade your Bliss Factor. Each task is designed to ultimately make you feel happier with your life—and these are things you can do for the rest of your life. I don't want you to look back and say, "Boy, that was one great month I had!" No way! I want you to take what you learn about yourself and your capacity for happiness and use those lessons each and every day going forward for decades to come.

You'll feel and see results—a sense of calm, a smile you can't wipe off your face, and suddenly others in your life will start asking, "Hey, what's your secret?" Your answer is simple: Bliss.

The Bliss Promise

Of course, life has its ups and downs, but my goal is get your Bliss Factor at a number that has you thriving day to day no matter what life throws at you. While I can't promise that life won't get hectic and even feel out of control sometimes, I can promise you that if you put your mind to it and dedicate yourself to following my plan, you will increase your Bliss Factor by at least ten points.

Bliss Pact with Yourself

I know you're itching to get started—and I'm just as excited as you are! Before you dive into the routine, I want you to learn all the ins and outs of why and how *Bliss Happens* works.

There's something else I feel compelled to mention right now—I love to laugh, and I love to make other people laugh. This isn't some boring self-help book guaranteed to have you snoring and drooling in the first page of a chapter. I fully hope and expect you to giggle, guffaw, and possibly snort (snorting is especially encouraged) while you learn about Bliss. But it's not *just* about a good chuckle—there's some serious life-changing stuff here that could make a huge difference in your life if you let it. That's why I felt compelled to create a little pact. It's just a friendly agreement between you and, well, you. Don't enter into it lightly though, dolls—after all, your Bliss is on the line here!

Bliss Pact

- ◎ I commit myself, over the next six weeks, to take my Bliss seriously.
- ◎ I recognize that I can't learn this stuff by osmosis; I have to actually read the book and implement the Bliss Plan in my life for it to work.
- ◎ I pledge allegiance to my happiness and the state of my home and lifestyle. In other words, I will be loyal to myself and do my best not to abandon my Bliss.
- ◎ I accept that life will never be perfect, and I'm more than OK with that. But I promise to do my best to take things in stride and not cry over spilled smoothies (or other daily incidents like goopy mascara or bright red pimples).
- ◎ I promise to wake up each morning and choose Bliss over the blues. I believe that it is a choice, and only I can decide this for myself.

Signature (no notary required): _____

Date: _____

Congratulations! You're on your way to increasing your Bliss Factor. I'm proud of you. Now, take my hand and let's get going.

Chapter 2

Inner Bliss

The very first and most important step to boosting your Bliss Factor is to start on the inside by shifting your attitude. It's easier than you might think to start feeling inner contentment, and I'll give you simple exercises and things to think about in the Bliss Plan that will help you create this attitude shift. But in this chapter, I want to show you *why* this is such an important key to your overall Bliss.

Years ago, I was a regular expert guest on a cable show. I remember I was standing just off the set waiting for my segment to start when I looked up and noticed the head makeup artist making a beeline for me. Had I smeared my mascara? Smudged my lipstick? She sidled up next to me and said, "How do you do it?" Before I could start apologizing (for what, I had no idea), she said, "Kym, I have to ask you. I see women come in here with diamonds the size of golf balls and designer bags worth more than my mortgage, but it doesn't matter how much stuff they've got—none of them seem to be as happy as you. Every time you come in you've got this genuine smile on your face. What's your secret? I really want to know if there's something I can do to feel that way." I was taken aback. This wasn't anywhere on the list of possible things I thought she might say! It melted my heart and was so affirming. I told her how I think it's because I've always been grateful for what I have, I never take anything for granted, and I choose happiness every moment of every single day. Of course, I have rough patches—we all do. But those bumps don't rock my world because my Blissful attitude is rock-solid.

That experience taught me a couple of important lessons. Firstly, it's obvious to others when you're in Bliss. I didn't have some halo over my head or go up to that makeup artist, get in her face, and declare, "I'm Blissful! I love life!" I just showed up every day and found the positive in every situation that presented itself, and she couldn't help but feel it. People watch you when you're not watching, and they know when you're genuinely happy. The goal of being Blissful isn't primarily about how others will respond, but imagine how much that can work in your favor in all areas of your life—whether you're interviewing for jobs, chitchatting with other moms at school, or just trying to get along with your mother-in-law.

Secondly, I learned that Bliss really is a choice, and when you choose it, something happens in your brain. Your brain releases a flood of endorphins in response to various types and degrees of pleasure. And when I decide to put a smile on my face and focus on the positive in my life rather than get caught up in the day-to-day petty stuff (traffic, that mother-in-law, an annoying boss, misbehaving children), I swear I can feel joy just take over my whole body. That's what I want for you! And I'm here to help you get it.

But choosing Bliss isn't just about opting for the high road. It's also about knowing what makes you happy and going after it, no matter what obstacles get in your way. Yes, sometimes you have to shift your plan a little, but more often than not, you just have to fight a little harder to achieve your goal. Recently, I saw this lesson embodied in Hunter, my 14-year-old son.

Hunter is the quarterback of his football team. After achieving early success in the sport, he was scouted by a competitive sports school in the Los Angeles area. (Yes, I know he is only 14, but that's pretty common in kids' sports nowadays.) He was up against four other quarterbacks, all of whom had played just as well and trained just as hard as my son. Because of a series of events, it ultimately came down to Hunter and one other young man. After weeks of trying them both out, training them, and pitting them against one another, the coach determined that they were equally talented.

The other boy became the first-string quarterback. But Hunter wasn't discouraged. He decided that, no matter what, he was only going to try harder and not walk away. That wasn't an easy decision for him, I'm sure. But with each practice, each training session, and each workout, he gave 110 percent and continued to hone his skills. I was so inspired watching him race to practice every day, work hard, and then stand on the sideline. And when game day rolled around, he continued to sit on the bench.

Hunter was patient. He knew in his heart that an opportunity would arise and he just had to wait for it. And then, it happened. During the course of a big game against a really tough school, the starting quarterback suffered a minor injury, and he had to sit out. (Don't worry—he's just fine!) The coach sent Hunter into the game, and the kid played with all of his heart. He had been training and preparing for this moment all day every day for months, and he was not going to let his chance at Bliss pass him by. He was going to grab it with both hands and hold on—which is exactly what he did as he threw that football to all the right receivers at all the right moments, leading their team to sweet victory.

He was the starting quarterback for the rest of that season because he continued to work hard and prove himself on that field. He didn't give up when the times were tough and he was being overlooked.

What do you do when you feel like you're being passed by? Do you try harder or walk away? Do you act like a victim and have resentment toward others, or do you resolve to work harder to reach your goal? Keep in mind, I'm not a psychologist. But I am an expert at what works for me and what I've seen work (or *not* work) for so many people in my life. The happiest people I know are the ones who follow these simple dos and don'ts of Bliss:

DO practice being grateful. It's not just saying "thank you" to the clerk in the store (though I do think that's important). Having a grateful attitude means you appreciate what you have. So, if your bank account isn't as full as you would like, you find ways to be thankful for the money you do have, and you get excited when you stretch every penny further than ever. I'm going to show you tons of ways to do that in this book! And it's not just about money. You will learn how to appreciate your body even if it's not perfect (because no one's is—even those models in the magazines who get airbrushed don't really look like that), your intellect, your strength, your face, your hair...the list goes on and on! I want you to get excited over even the little victories in life because they are victories nonetheless. Notice them. Maybe it's just the fact that your little one went to sleep early or that you have a roof over your head or clean water to drink. Pick something, anything, that you're grateful for, and think about it for a moment. You can't help but smile, right? You can do that all day; it never gets old, and the payoff always works.

DO give Bliss away as much as you receive it. I am a firm believer that the more you give of yourself to others, the more happiness you get back. But try not to think of it like a mutual fund, where you invest some money and then expect to make more. It doesn't really work if you're giving it away just so you get more in return. Instead, make a conscious effort to find joy in the actual process of giving. When I am feeling down or having a rough day, I make myself find something positive about every situation I'm in that day and every person I encounter. Say there's a store clerk who kind of has an attitude; I'll quickly scan her up and down and realize I adore her shoes. Rather than focus on her nasty attitude, I compliment her fabulous taste in shoes and then walk away. I don't know about her, but I end up feeling better. It shifts the whole mood, energy, and environment in that store. Positive reaps positive. I'm not saying you have to donate large sums of money to a charitable organization or volunteer in the middle of the night at a homeless shelter. Giving Bliss away can be as simple as adding coins to a stranger's parking meter, paying for the person behind you on the toll road, or thanking a soldier for fighting for our freedom. It could even be as subtle as smiling at a stranger. I'm telling you, these little gifts of Bliss go a long way—both for you and for the recipient. And call me cheesy, but I think they also make the world a happier, kinder place.

DO set realistic goals. Perhaps you've defined your Bliss as being just like Kate Hudson and Beyoncé. They are gorgeous, talented, and very famous young women. And, I'm sorry, but you can't be them... those positions have been filled. But why not try to become the Rachel McAdams of your local theater group? Or the Alicia Keys of your community choir? I'm serious, you guys! There are so many ways to use your natural talents and share them with others. This applies to every area of your life. For instance, if you want your home to look like the pages of a Pottery Barn catalog but you can't afford so much as a candle from there, find realistic ways to still make your home gorgeous. There are so many hidden gems at local flea markets, garage sales, and vintage or consignment shops that can make your home beautiful, with the added bonus that they are totally unique and far from cookie-cutter. When you're realistic about everything from your gene pool to your budget, you can set yourself up for success by finding surprising and creative ways to reach your goals. Your self-esteem will start to soar, and you will accomplish things you never thought you could.

DO envision your Bliss and hone it. How could you possibly ever get what your heart desires if you don't know what those desires are in the first place? That's why I want you to make a Bliss List. Get a notebook, one you really like looking at so you're even more encouraged to write in it, and put a title on the very first page that reads "I will be Blissful when...." Start off each entry with that open-ended line. Keep this list close to your heart, and write in it whenever you feel compelled to do so. With Bliss goals, it helps to be very specific. Just like you hear fitness experts say that if you focus on the muscle you're training and picture it getting stronger, you'll actually improve its performance. In the same way, the more you're able to spell out what you want, the more likely you are to follow through and make it happen. I interviewed a beautiful singer not long ago, and she had lost quite a bit of weight. When I asked her how she did it, I was half expecting her to tell me about a prescription diet pill or a personal chef who followed her around for months feeding her only organic carrots and blueberries. So, I was caught off guard when she told me that she had done it simply by writing down the weight she wanted to be and then recording every morsel of food she ate in a journal. She said, "If I bite it, I write it"...and it worked! The country-singing cutie was on to something. It makes perfect sense because she defined her goal clearly, and then she could physically see all the ways she was working to achieve the goal. Now, imagine what you can do with just pencil, paper, and purpose. (Kind of sounds like a country-western song. Wink!)

DO keep listening until you hear your inner voice. This is the voice that will be your guide and lead you to your place of Bliss. This is your God-given gift that will put you on the pathway. Sometimes it's just a gentle whisper, and you have to turn off all the outer noise like the television or radio in order to hear it. Or, this might mean shutting off all the other voices in your head that drown out your inner whisper. You know what I'm talking about—the constant day-to-day inner monologue about everything from what you need at the grocery store to berating yourself over the cake you wish you hadn't eaten. Find ways to hit mute on all that chatter and just listen to what's left. Hear that? That murmur is a little slice of Bliss, and the volume can get even louder if you'll work at it.

DON'T focus on what you lack. If you spend all your time thinking about what you *don't* have, you will inevitably create a life that feels empty. When you see a woman walking across the street toting the newest Gucci bag, do you get a flash of envy? In that moment, ask yourself what would happen if you got that Gucci bag. Would the stars align, angels sing, and your life suddenly become complete? Would that handbag bring you deep, lasting Bliss? Or would it be more like a little "hit" of Bliss, a temporary satisfaction that fades as soon as the next moment of emptiness or envy hits you once again? I find that the more material things people get, the more they want, and they reach a point where nothing is ever enough. If you're focusing on what you lack, you're blocking your own path to Bliss, and you might even be creating a greed monster. If you just said, "But, Kym, I *deserve* that Gucci bag," then I say, "You deserve more than what that bag can offer you. You deserve Bliss. Let me help you find it!" It's not the pursuit of happiness that will get you to your Bliss—it's the happiness of the pursuit!

DON'T make excuses. I used to hold a title that I wasn't very proud of. It was the Queen of Excuses. This is a surefire way to sabotage your Bliss. Maybe you use your busy schedule as an excuse for why you can't focus on your health, your looks, your home, or your happiness. But I'll show you how these things don't have to be time-intensive—there are so many ways to incorporate them seamlessly into your chaotic life. Or maybe your excuses are in the financial vein, like "I can't afford to be beautiful." That's my favorite one because I'm going to show you how your beauty budget can actually be combined with your grocery budget, of all things. I'm known for my 59-cent beauty tricks. Some of the treatments in this book are as cheap as a kiwi! Come on, you can afford a kiwi.

DON'T be too hard on you. I think we women are guilty of this partially because society expects us all to be superwomen and partially because we're just innately critical of ourselves. We are supposed to juggle it all—keep those plates spinning while running miles in high heels. Listen here, sister: In order to raise your Bliss Factor, you have to cut yourself some slack. The next time you look in the mirror and words like *fat*, *old*, or *ugly* cross your mind, ask yourself this question: Would you ever consider looking at your child, your best friend, or your mother and saying those words, calling them those mean, nasty names that you call yourself? I think not. You don't want to hurt them like that, and they wouldn't stick around and listen to it anyway! You probably build them up with encouraging things like, "Hey, you look great, Aunt Helen! Have you lost weight?" Those positive affirmations just fly right out of your mouth when they're aimed at someone you love—but shouldn't you be loving and encouraging yourself most of all? We end up being our own worst, meanest critic. That all stops right here, right now. The next time you criticize yourself in that mirror, I want you to throw your shoulders back, toss your hair around, and say out loud, "You look pretty darn good" and walk out of the room. Even if you aren't feeling all that good about your body, say it anyway. Find something you do like about yourself—and zero in on that. Soon enough, it'll start to sink in. And as you apply the lessons from this book, congratulate yourself on even the smallest accomplishments along the way.

Trust Your Inner Bliss

Honing your inner Bliss isn't easy; taking risks and trusting that it will all work out takes guts. But if Bliss were easy to find, everyone would have it! I want to share with you a story that is very near and dear to my heart—it's the story of how I met and ultimately married my husband of 27 years, Jerry. It's kind of an *Against All Odds* story, not a *Bold & Beautiful* love story, but that's what I like the most about it.

I was 22 years old and barely out of school. I had graduated college on a Friday, and on Monday I started working as the co-anchor of the noon, 6 p.m., and 11 p.m. news in Marquette, Michigan. I was living my dream: I had always wanted to report the news, and even though tiny little Marquette wasn't really on the map, so to speak, nearby Detroit's news stations had millions of viewers. I felt like I was right on track to becoming the next Jessica Savitch or Diane Sawyer.

Well, my perfect little plan that I'd devised for my life started to go to hell in a handbasket when I landed an interview with Jerry Douglas, the big-time soap star who played John Abbott on *The Young and the Restless* (insert dramatic soap opera music here). Our meeting was kind of like a fairytale...every day when I sat at the news desk waiting to begin the noon news, I would watch the last 15 minutes of *Y&R* on the monitors since that was what aired right before our news program. I knew exactly who John, er, Jerry was—I mean, he was practically the glue that held Genoa City together! (OK, nonsoaps fans, I'll cease with the references to the show now.) I was also an avid reader of all the gossip magazines and *Soap Opera Digest*. Almost exactly one month before I was given the assignment to interview Jerry, I was enjoying a mini vacation from the rain and snow at the local newsstand when my eyes fell on a picture of him. The hair on the back of my neck stood up, but it wasn't just his dashing good looks that caused that reaction. It was because I knew in that instant, without even the tiniest doubt in my mind that I was going to meet that man someday. I held on to the magazine and wondered how it could ever be possible that me, Kym, a news reporter in middle-of-nowhere, frozen tundra Michigan with two people and a polar bear in my studio audience, could ever meet a Hollywood soap star (the odds aren't even measurable!), but I never once questioned the truth that my inner voice was telling me.

Thirty days later, when my boss told me that I'd be interviewing Jerry Douglas while he was passing through on his way to Canada for a charity event, I felt a strange mixture of emotions: I was both shocked and not at all surprised. After all, this is the man who just one month ago I'd known for sure I was going to meet! The interview couldn't have gone better—we laughed the whole time, and he was perfectly charming, funny, and sweet. He even took me and the whole crew out to dinner afterward. He left for Canada the next morning, and I lamented over the undeniable fact that I'd never see him again. Sigh.

I settled back into life as usual, bundled up in my winter coat, my brush with the enchanting Hollywood star over for good. As I walked into work, the newsroom seemed to be atwitter about something. Had a big news story hit, I wondered? But when I rounded the corner and saw a bigger-than-life basket filled with no less than 300 red, long-stemmed roses, I was stunned. I found out later it had taken the combined efforts of every florist in town to put together this massive bouquet, if you can even call it that, at the request of Mr. Jerry Douglas. And my name was on the card. Sure, I had received thank-you gifts after an interview in the past. It was the whole "you don't ask me any tough or embarrassing questions on TV, and I'll send you a couple yellow daffodils" routine. Only this time, the daffodils got an upgrade... big time.

This was my big Hollywood romance moment, and I was relishing it. That is, until it became a story in one of those gossip magazines

I always loved to read. That's right; the *National Enquirer* got ahold of the "soap star sends small town girl 300 roses" story. Wow—I guess that's one way to move my TV career along, but I was freaking out. Don't worry, there wasn't anything sleazy going on, certainly no tabloid-caliber activity (although I'm sure they wished there was!). Personally, I think they printed it just because the whole thing sounded like a scene in a soap opera playing out in real life. I saved the article and still have it in a scrapbook.

Final scene: Jerry and I spoke on the phone for a few months, and our relationship grew and flourished. I knew in my heart that I'd found my soul mate, no matter how crazy or unexpected the pathway had been. On paper, we were all wrong for each other. Twenty-something years difference in our ages, living totally different lives on opposite sides of the country...the list of "why this could never work" was a mile long! I'm sure my parents wondered why I couldn't just stay the course there in Michigan, marry a nice Midwestern boy, and have lots of babies. But I listened to my inner voice and let it lead the way. I trusted what I knew to be true, and I took a crazy risk by packing up, quitting my anchor job in Marquette, and moving to Los Angeles. We were married 18 months later, and we will celebrate 30 years soon.

We all know real life is no soap opera. The journey isn't over just because you've found your Bliss in the form of your soul mate. Maintaining your inner Bliss on a daily basis is where the real challenge lies. Jerry and I have come across many bumps in the road, and our love has been tested; after all, every day can't be a "300 roses" day! But despite the challenges thrown at us, from a divorce in his past to relationships with stepchildren, pressures of the entertainment industry, and even struggles with infertility, we've always been each other's strength.

Does it feel like the Bliss deck is stacked against you and the odds are almost never in your favor? Don't let the rough patches shake your foundation and rob you of your Bliss. Hold on tightly to the belief that you can be happy again. What is your goal? What is your inner voice telling you? Maybe it wasn't a picture in a soap magazine that made the hairs on your neck stand up, but I'm guessing you've had a moment of realization. And if you haven't, listen harder. We'll all be tested, and we'll all endure trials, but I believe if you choose Bliss every single day, search for it, and seek it out, that you'll soon understand those obstacles help you grow and are all part of the journey.

. . .

As you read on and begin my Bliss Plan, keep these basic principles of Inner Bliss in mind because they apply across the board, not only to every chapter in this book but to every chapter of your life.

Part 2

Beauty Bliss

Hello, gorgeous. Yes, that's *you*! We've all heard that beauty is in the eye of the beholder. Well, get ready to behold some serious beauty every time you catch a glimpse of yourself in a mirror. I'm going to show you how you can have glowing skin, a whiter smile, bright eyes, healthy nails, shiny hair, and a great body without spending all of your hard-earned cash. The very first step is to believe that you can be a drop-dead, stunning, knockout. Don't worry, I'll help you do that too.

My secret is what I like to call "two-for-one beauty and fun." I'll share with you foods that enhance your beauty when you eat them or when you apply them to your skin, face, nails, or hair. I'll also reveal household items you can use to firm and tone your body. That's right; you can do more than just sweep the floors with that broom! And the "fun" comes into play because I guarantee you'll have plenty of it while doing all of these treatments and knowing you're saving cash all the while. Listen, I'm not a regular guest on *Ellen* because I take myself seriously all the time—I'm on there because this stuff is hysterical, but it still works! That's no accident.

So many of us have to make financial sacrifices, and very often the first thing to go is the beauty budget. No longer. That's because my two-for-one beauty and fun treatments are comprised primarily of ingredients either you already have in your house (particularly in your kitchen) or you can purchase inexpensively at your grocery store. So, now rather than having a separate beauty budget you usually spend at the mall, splurge on at a spa, or use to order products online, you can combine your beauty budget with your grocery budget and look better than ever. Plus, there's the added bonus that you're exposing yourself to fewer harsh chemicals because you'll be trading products made in a lab with mostly natural foods you would eat anyway!

I believe beauty comes from the inside out and the outside in, but let's get specific and talk about the inside for a moment. Before we begin with all of the fun, outrageous, and highly effective Beauty Bliss treatments in the following chapters, I'd like to turn your attention to a few essential vitamins and minerals that you should consider taking because they enhance your natural splendor. (Always talk to your doc before starting a new vitamin regimen, darling.) My physician always tells me that my body absorbs nutrients best when it comes from the food that I eat, and in Chapter 7, "Body Bliss," you'll find all kinds of healthy mood-boosting foods that will also nourish your body. But just in case your typical frenzied day barely allows for you to scarf down a fiber bar at lunch and a frozen dinner before bed, it's a good idea to stock up on supplements.

Beauty Bliss Supplement List

At this juncture I'd like to remind you that I'm not a doctor and I don't even play one on TV! This advice is simply what has worked for me and what I've researched, but I implore you to chat with your own physician about which vitamins, minerals, and supplements he or she recommends specifically for you. Everyone is different! In general, the following are the supplements that I believe can truly make a difference in our skin, hair, nails and every other aspect of our overall gorgeousness:

Vitamins A and C: These are antioxidants, and they are your friends when it comes to having beautiful, glowing skin (not to mention a slim waistline and overall healthy disposition).

Protein: If it's long, luscious locks you're after, protein is the answer because your hair needs plenty of it to grow. If you're deficient in protein, the strands of your hair can actually weaken—and guess what else?—they can lose their color. No joke! Protein also helps repair skin cells that have been damaged over time. No, you are not damaged goods, but sometimes pollution, sun exposure, and, yes, even aging can cause damage. Whether it's adding some grilled chicken to your Waldorf salad, sipping a whey protein shake on your way to work, or scrambling up some eggs, make sure you're eating protein.

Omega-3 Fatty Acids: Maybe you've read about these or your doctor has told you to take fish-oil supplements—well, there are good reasons for all the buzz. Omega 3s are found in fish like salmon or supplements like flax seed, and when you're getting enough of them, you'll notice your skin is softer and healthier looking, your scalp is naturally moisturized (no flakes!), and your lips are less likely to get chapped. (I even add flax-seed oil to my dog food to help Brady, my dog, with dry skin woes!)

Iron: If you're deficient in iron (anemic), you might look pale, your nails may break more easily, and you could even—gasp—experience thinning hair. Make sure your multivitamin includes iron, ladies.

One more thing before we do a graceful swan dive into all things Beauty Bliss related. In the next few chapters, you'll find many treatments that include some aspect of coconuts. I just wanted to let you know why I'm cuckoo for coconuts and why you soon will be too!

Why I'm Cuckoo for Coconuts

There are so many reasons to love this crazy fruit! You'll discover various parts of the coconut listed as ingredients in many of my remedies. Here is a behind-the-scenes glimpse at what makes coconuts so fabulous:

Coconut Water: Maybe you've noticed, in recent years, how the coconut-water industry (which hardly existed five years ago) has truly exploded. Well, there's good reason for that. This thirst-quenching H_2O comes from young, green coconuts. By sipping on just one 46-calorie cup of this goodness, you'll fortify your body with 600 milligrams of potassium, which is almost 200 milligrams more than a banana! And you want plenty of potassium because it plays a big role in hydration, and it can even reduce fluid retention. More hydration and less retention means a flatter tummy, depuffed eyes, and no unsightly cankles! I use it in my morning smoothies all the time, and you know me by now...if it's good enough to drink, it's good enough to put on your skin! You'll find this in my dry skin treatments because it hydrates from the outside too.

Coconut Milk: There's a nearly magical substance in coconut milk called lauric acid, which is a type of saturated fat, and it is a fantastic conditioner for your hair. It adds so much shine and volume that you might just empty your conditioner bottle and fill it with coconut milk instead! Oh, and they make low-calorie versions now, so it's a healthy and delicious addition to smoothies too.

Coconut Oil: High in vitamins E and K and healthy saturated fat, coconut oil is great for deeply moisturizing dry skin, hair, and nails. I love using a little dab of it at night on my face so I can wake up looking soft and hydrated. It's also great to use a tiny bit when cooking; I like to mix up the types of oils I cook with, and this one is definitely in my repertoire!

OK, let's get gorgeous!

Chapter 3

Skin Bliss

I'm definitely not a dermatologist, and yet I get more questions from women about how to improve their skin than anything else! It's understandable, since we all want to look youthful. From smoothing out smile lines to erasing adult acne and abolishing age spots (I like to call them "freckles on steroids"), keeping your skin looking beautiful is doable, affordable, and definitely worth the effort.

What's the Skinny on Skin?

Before you can wrap your head around what can make your facial skin look like it belongs on the cover of Glamour magazine, you really should know a few basic facts.

There's a layer of fat under all of the skin on your body, but that layer is a lot thinner on your facial skin. Because you don't have this lovely fat layer to plump out the skin and keep it smooth, you're more likely to get visible wrinkles on your face. Perfect. The one place fat would seriously come in handy, and it's not there! But now it makes sense why plastic surgeons and dermatologists often inject fat under the skin on people's faces, right? I have another newsflash for you: That thinner layer of fat under your facial skin also makes you more vulnerable to the sun's harsh rays, which can cause age spots, wrinkles, and other unsightly facial flaws. That's why you want to wear sunscreen on your face practically 24/7! I keep at least SPF 15 on my face all the time; usually it's part of my daily moisturizer or makeup foundation. I always go for the organic stuff because otherwise it can be laden with lots of chemicals and potential toxins.

The Ultimate Beauty-on-a-Budget Chart

Maybe you've wondered what secret formula scientists have created in a faraway lab and then stuffed inside a beautiful 1-ounce glass bottle and put on sale—well, it's hardly on "sale" since it can cost a fortune!—at the local cosmetic counter of your spa. Well, the answers are here, my beauty budgeters! In the left column of this chart, you'll find some of the most popular and widely used active ingredients from high-end skin products. In the middle column, you'll see the benefits these ingredients provide to your skin. The right column is where the magic happens. Believe it or not, many of these ingredients come from natural, healthy, and far less expensive foods or products. Hey, if it's good enough to eat, it's good enough for your face!

Now, before someone from one of the high-end cosmetics companies sends me a letter, let me be clear. The little jars, bottles, and pumps are filled with products that have these ingredients in a higher concentration, so you may get faster results from using them. But if you're diligent, using the natural substitutes will very often give you similar results, and you can also take comfort in knowing that you can pronounce every ingredient that you're putting onto your face! You'll also find many of these ingredients in the skin treatments within this chapter.

INGREDIENTS	BENEFITS	NATURAL SUBSTITUTE
Alpha-hydroxy acids: 1. Citric acid 2. Lactic acid 3. Malic acid 4. Tartaric acid 5. Glycolic acid	Exfoliates and hydrates skin, smooths fine lines, improves skin tone, and cleanses pores.	1. Kiwi, lemon, lime, orange, grapefruit 2. Milk and yogurt 3. Apples 4. Grapes 5. Sugar cane and brown sugar
Retinol	Type of vitamin A that promotes collagen production and reduces fine lines by plumping skin. Also helps improve skin color.	Butter Milk Buttermilk Eggs
Beta-hydroxy acid: Salicylic acid	Improves texture of skin by exfoliating. Penetrates pores and reduces blackheads and whiteheads.	Aspirin Strawberries
Hydroquinone	Skin-lightening ingredient. Reduces dark spots and age spots by decreasing melanin formation in the skin.	Hydroquinone isn't in any foods, but lemon juice has many of the same benefits to your skin.
Alpha-lipoic acid	Antioxidant that helps fight skin damage and free radicals, repair damage, reduce fine lines, reduce pores, and exfoliate.	Red meat, beets, spinach, yeast (particularly brewer's yeast)

Aside from wrinkles and sun damage, quite a few things can go haywire with the skin on your face. That's great if you're in the skin-care industry, considering women spend a whopping $80 billion annually on products that promise to fight aging, such as tonics, creams, gels, lotions, balms, serums, spot treatments, exfoliants, microdermabrasion kits, and much, much more. And I'm not even including the hundreds of expensive spa facial treatments, lasers, peels—oh my gosh—the list doesn't end! But you know what? I don't want one penny of those billions to come out of your handbag. There are just so many inexpensive, more natural (and healthier!) ways to make your skin look great.

Skin Snafu: Wrinkles

When George Clooney smiles on the silver screen, your heart just lights up, and you probably smile too, right? The last thing on your mind (and his!) is how his crow's feet and other facial lines suddenly deepen and become more visible when he grins from ear to ear. But when you look in the mirror or at photos of yourself, the very first thing you notice are your lines—it's as though there's a magnifying glass just zooming in on them. You may think, "Hold the phone...is that a new wrinkle between my eyes? I swear it wasn't there last week! That's it. Life is over. I am officially old." I have two points: First, don't begrudge Clooney or any man just because gray hair and wrinkles seem to only add to their sex appeal. File that under the "Good for them" category. It may not be fair, but like I said, good for them. Second, you're too hard on yourself! I have a third point, too: We can reduce those wrinkles and prevent more from forming without spending a fortune. Life is most assuredly not over.

Before we get started, I have to tell you about an email I received from a woman who confided that she'd been trying not to laugh anymore because she didn't want her laugh lines to get any worse. This woman went to great lengths to avoid cracking up all in the name of beauty! Her refusal to laugh, giggle, or even smile too broadly actually was causing social awkwardness and practically putting her in a depression! Can you imagine? I mean, not smiling or laughing probably ages us more than anything else! It's definitely not worth all that. Laughter is highly encouraged on the Bliss Plan, so let me show you how you can have it all.

Ooh-La-La Lavender Pore Cleanser

WHAT YOU NEED

4 cups of water

8 drops of lavender oil

You'll see this sumptuous steam treatment in a lot of my skin recipes. You can find lavender essential oil for less than $10 at most health food stores. Even if that seems like a lot for a little bottle, you'll never need more than a few drops per treatment because it's pretty potent and it will last you a while. I love it when a little goes a long way, don't you? Plus, I'll share dozens of uses for this exceptionally versatile oil, so you'll be glad to have it on hand. This simple yet luxurious treat for your skin is sure to keep it soft and glowing. The steam opens up your pores, so whatever product or treatment you use afterward will soak right in and work more efficiently.

WHAT YOU DO

Simply bring the water to a gentle boil on the stove until it begins producing steam. Add eight drops of lavender oil to the water. Make sure your skin is clean, with no makeup. Put your face in the steam but not so close that you risk getting splashed with the boiling water. Put it just get close enough so your skin can drink up the moisture from the steam. Stay put for about five to seven minutes. Your skin is saying "Thank you!"

OPTIONAL: Put a towel over your head and the pot of water so the steam can't escape as easily.

Skin Treatment #1:
The Lean, Mean, Green Wrinkle Cream

WHAT YOU NEED:

Bowl and spoon

Half an avocado (or leafy green veggies)

1 tablespoon olive oil

I make this anti-wrinkle cream treatment with avocados because they're rich in folic acid, which is a type of B vitamin. Your skin loves folic acid because it helps fight sun damage and protects your cells.

WHAT YOU DO

First, perform my *Ooh-La-La Lavender Pore Cleanser* on clean skin to get your pores ready for this wrinkle-shrinking remedy. Next, mix together the avocado with the olive oil in a blender or food processor until it's smooth and creamy (if you make it too chunky, the chunks will fall off your face easily). Then, gently massage the green goodness into your face and neck so that all your skin except your eyelids and the area below your eyes are covered. (Feel free to munch on the leftover avocado, since it is high in fiber and healthy fats and very filling.) You might want to wrap a towel around your neck and shoulders to catch any drips! Leave it on for 15 minutes, and then rinse with warm water.

SUBSTITUTES: I know avocados can be a little on the pricey side, and they're not always easy to find, so you can substitute any green leafy vegetable. Just dab a little olive oil on one side of the leaves and apply them to your face. Remove after 15 minutes. (If you can splurge, however, the added benefit of avocados is that they're high in fatty acids too, which helps your skin produce more collagen.)

That's a simple and very effective wrinkle treatment, but there's more! I recommend doing it once a week and then doing *The Cabbage Patch Anti-Wrinkle Mask* a couple of days later.

Skin Treatment #2:
The Cabbage Patch Anti-Wrinkle Mask

WHAT YOU NEED

1 head of cabbage

1 teaspoon honey

1/4 teaspoon brewer's yeast

You may have heard of or even used expensive vitamin C serums before. Vitamin C is a powerful antioxidant, so its mission in life is to fight free radicals and thus protect your skin cells. Doctors want you to eat plenty of vitamin C, and I want you to put plenty of it on your face! Cabbage has vitamin C as well as folic acid and beta carotene, so it's a main ingredient in this mask. Brewer's yeast, also in this recipe, is a well-kept secret in the skin care world. This stuff is seriously amazing, and I'm not talking about its role in making beer. It's very high in selenium and several types of B vitamins, and it can help with all kinds of skin issues. The final ingredient is honey, which has wonderful healing properties for the skin. I've even used it on minor cuts and scrapes to speed up healing!

WHAT YOU DO

Put two to three cabbage leaves in a food processor or blender for a few seconds, until they're almost like a wet paste. They create a "juice" when ground up, and that's the part you really want to use, but you can use the ground-up leaves too. Mix the paste or juice with the honey and brewer's yeast. Apply to your clean face and neck, avoiding the eye area. Leave for 20 minutes, and then gently rinse it off. I know it may not be the most aromatic treatment, but sometimes beauty is smelly!

Skin Snafu: Age Spots

When you were a kid, your mom may have told you how adorable the freckles on your nose were. Maybe as you got older, you even learned to embrace them. And then, one day, maybe in your late 20s, a rather oversized freckle made its debut on your cheek. As you examined it closer, you realized—gasp!—it's not a freckle at all. It's an age spot, and it's not adorable in the least! Horror of horrors.

The lighter your natural shade of skin, the more likely you are to develop these targeted areas of darkened pigmentation (that sounds better than age spot, right?), and you can address your thank-you letter to the sun. (But you're also to blame if you're not wearing sunblock regularly.) I have fantastic news for you, though. They are not permanent. They're only there for as long as you don't treat them, and that treatment need not require a call to an expensive doctor's office.

Skin Treatment #3:
Lychee Lightening Facial

WHAT YOU NEED

1/2 can lychees (can also use *substitutes*)

2 tablespoons Greek yogurt

I know lychees (pronounced "lee-chee") might seem a little foreign, but they really are slippery little treasures in a can. These small fruits have more vitamin C than lemons, and they also boast high amounts of copper. Both vitamin C and copper are natural antioxidants that protect your skin from free radical damage and lighten dark pigmentation, such as age spots. You can find these gems either in cans or in jars at most grocery stores these days, but if your local market doesn't carry them, try an Asian market. They were originally grown and harvested in China, but as they've become more popular, there are more growers around the world. Maybe you've seen them on the drink menu at a fancy bar in the form of a martini. But we're not drinking them today; we're smearing them on our face! You can also do this treatment on your hands if you have a few speckles there.

WHAT YOU DO

First, perform my *Ooh-La-La Lavender Pore Cleanser* on your skin to get it fully prepared for this indulgence. Next, mash up the lychees with a fork or put them in the blender for a few seconds. Combine them with the Greek yogurt in a bowl. Over a sink, apply the mixture to your skin, avoiding your eye areas and lips. It may be a little runny, so drain off some of the liquid if necessary. Let it soak in for 10 to 15 minutes. To remove, you may first need to gently wipe off the chunks with tissue and then gently rinse your face with warm water. Dab on your favorite moisturizer or a tiny bit of coconut oil. Don't forget sunscreen before you go outside!

SUBSTITUTES: If lychees are too difficult to find in your area, you can substitute another fruit high in vitamin C such as kiwi, strawberries, or tangerines. You can even use a can of mandarin oranges.

If pigmentation is your skin woe, do the lychee lightening treatment once a week for your entire face and neck. For targeted spot treatment, the *"Try Not to Cry" Onion Spot Remover* is a magical mixture you can use daily. But if your skin starts to get really dry in the areas where you're using it, discontinue use for a week and use extra moisturizer. I can't stress enough the importance of slathering sunscreen on your skin when you're doing these treatments regularly since you're exposing fresh, new skin cells to the sun's harsh rays.

Skin Treatment #4:
The "Try Not to Cry" Onion Spot Remover

WHAT YOU NEED

1 tablespoon apple cider vinegar

2 teaspoons onion juice (either from a jar or you can mince up half an onion and then squeeze it through cheesecloth for fresh juice)

NOTE: Save the leftovers in a small, sealed container and store it in fridge.

Yes, I'm known for some pretty zany ideas about what to put on your face or hair, but this next one may have you wondering if I'm joking. I'm not! Onions are considered to be an anti-inflammatory food because of their flavonoid content, and they naturally bleach skin because of their acidic qualities. Much like you peel onions layers one by one, onion juice will exfoliate your skin and cause the thin top layers to flake off, which also means buh-bye to your darkened pigmentation.

Mixed together with the lightening power of apple cider vinegar, this treatment packs a one-two punch to age spots. You don't want to treat your entire face with this, because it will lighten all pigmentation, as opposed to just the age spot that you want to blend in with the rest of your skin. Onions aren't as acidic as lemons, so this is something you can do daily without running as high a risk of drying out your skin.

WHAT YOU DO

The ratio should be one part apple cider vinegar to two parts onion juice. Dip a cotton swab or cotton ball into the mixture and hold it right on the age spot. Hold it on there for a few seconds. Wait 10 to 15 minutes before rinsing it off with warm water. (As silly as it may look, you can wear a pair of airtight swimming goggles when you're doing this treatment so the smell doesn't make you cry.)

Skin Treatment #5:
Old Timey Buttermilk Spot Wash

WHAT YOU NEED

1 cup buttermilk (you can make this by mixing dried buttermilk and water together, or you can buy it fresh)

We're not making pancakes, ladies; we're lightening your age spots with some good old-fashioned buttermilk! It has lactic acid in it, which is a common ingredient in fancy spa-quality skin peels because it can lighten and brighten your beautiful skin so it simply glows.

WHAT YOU DO

This is so simple that you have no reason not to do this often! In fact, I do a buttermilk wash at least twice a week. Apply buttermilk (using a soft sponge or a makeup brush) to your face, being careful not to let it drip in your eyes. Leave it on for 10 minutes, and then rinse with warm water.

Splish Splash...You Put What in the Bath? The Buttermilk Soak

Who doesn't love a warm, luxurious bath? Instead of carelessly tossing in whatever liquid soap you have lying around, consider taking a double-duty buttermilk bath. This combination of dried buttermilk (you can also use fresh) and Epsom salts make for a dynamic duo to help moisturize dry skin and decrease your water retention, not to mention how relaxed this will make you feel. Buttermilk, take me away!

Mix together 2 cups of dried buttermilk and 2 cups of Epsom salts, and pour them into a bathtub full of warm water (put directly into running water for fast dissolving). For extra foam, add another cup of buttermilk. Include a few drops of lavender essential oil for an even more calming experience...I get sleepy just writing about it...zzzz....

Skin Snafu: Adult Acne

Silly rabbit, acne is for kids, isn't it? We all wish! Actually, more than half of adult women will find themselves fighting pimples once again as an unwelcomed reliving of our youth. As we stare at our reflection, we're reminded of the relentless teasing: "Ew, look at crater face Kym over there!" Or, "Hey, pizza face! Get some Clearasil!" Adults may not be so outwardly cruel, but we worry what everyone is thinking just the same.

Acne strikes us as adults for many reasons like hormonal shifts, stress, and more. I do think it's smart to talk to your dermatologist if you have more than just a pimple here and there, just to see whether there might be something more serious going on in your body.

Some women mistakenly think that if they're suffering with acne it's because their skin is super oily. The truth is that many breakouts occur when your skin is too dry because your oil glands go into overdrive trying to produce oil to make up for the desert dryness. My overall tip is to be wise and moisturize, even if you're currently at odds with a pimple or two. The more you can take the reins and add healthy moisture to your skin, the less work your oil glands have to do and the less likely you are to break out.

For the occasional breakout, these are some fantastic natural treatments that will send those zits packing.

Skin Treatment #6:
Pizza Facial for Pizza Face

WHAT YOU NEED

1 clove garlic, minced

1/4 cup tomato paste

Take your skin from extra pepperoni to cheese only with this pizza facial. Tomatoes are acidic, so they help exfoliate, but they also have antioxidants like vitamin C and vitamin A to help fight damage like acne scarring. Garlic is a natural antibiotic, so when you apply it on pimples, it helps to kill the bacteria in the skin and speed up healing of the blemish. You should do this every other day during a breakout.

WHAT YOU DO

First, perform my *Ooh-La-La Lavender Pore Cleanser* on clean skin to get your pores ready for this anti-acne fix. Then, put the garlic clove in the food processor along with the tomato paste, and blend until it's smooth. Paint the mixture evenly on your face, avoiding the eye areas. Leave on for 10 minutes, and then rinse off with warm water.

NOTE: If you don't have time for the full treatment, simply hold one peeled clove of garlic directly to blemishes for a minute or two.

If prevention is more your game right now, here's a great mask you can apply once a week to keep zits from cropping up when you least expect them.

Skin Treatment #7:
The Berry Blemish Blocker

WHAT YOU NEED

1 handful strawberries

1 tablespoon honey

I love strawberries and use them all the time. They are seriously amazing! One of their many amazing qualities is that they contain salicylic acid. If you've ever had acne, you know that many over-the-counter acne treatments contain salicylic acid because it's known to clear up pimples by taking down the swelling and redness. It also prevents future breakouts. As for honey, it has antimicrobial enzymes; when you put it on your skin, it can actually choke out the bacteria causing the zits because they can't survive in all that natural sugar. It's kind of crazy how well this works.

WHAT YOU DO
Put the strawberries in a blender or food processor, and blend until smooth. Mix in the honey, and apply the mixture to your clean skin, avoiding the eye areas. (If there's any leftover, don't throw it away—eat it! I think it tastes delicious with a cup of yogurt.) Leave for just 15 minutes, and then rinse off with warm water. Do this routine once or twice a week, and before you know it, zits will be a thing of your past, just like embarrassing yearbook pictures!

Skin Snafu: Dry Skin

Right this second, the cells in your skin are probably screaming with their tiny little voices, "Moisture! I need moisture!" They can't ever get too much of it. Keeping your skin moisturized not only helps treat and prevent the look and feeling of dryness but also helps your cells perform at their very best to fight off free radicals, pollution, and other vicious outsiders trying to steal your beauty away.

If you're dry, remember my *Moisturizer Advisor* information, and start following that advice ASAP! And to get some immediate moisture into your skin, try this treatment today.

Moisturizer Advisor

Finding a moisturizer that's right for your skin can be as arduous as searching for a mate (well, not quite, but you get my drift). Think of all the moisturizers to choose from in the beauty aisle at the grocery store, the sea of cosmetics counters at the mall, and the glitzy glass shelves at the spa—it's overwhelming, no? You finally agree to go on a blind date with one, only to find out it leaves you feeling greasy and disgruntled instead of blissful. To help narrow your options and increase your odds of moisturizer success, here's my advice:

SKIN TYPE	INGREDIENTS TO LOOK FOR	INGREDIENTS TO AVOID
Normal skin	Water-based moisturizer containing lightweight oils, such as cetyl alcohol, or silicone-derived ingredients, such as cyclomethicone. Lanolin (an emollient) fills spaces between skin cells, smoothing the surface of the skin.	**Parabens:** Watch out for parabens such as methyl, propyl, butyl, and ethyl. These are used as preservatives to prevent bacteria from growing in the bottle and to extend shelf life. They can cause allergic reactions and rashes.
Oily skin	Water-based products labeled "noncomedogenic," which means they won't clog your pores.	**Propylene glycol:** This is an oil-free product that is drying and can sting irritated skin.

Skin Treatment #8:
Coconut Hydro Skin Infusion

WHAT YOU NEED

2 tablespoons coconut water (unflavored)

8 flat cotton round pads

SKIN TYPE	INGREDIENTS TO LOOK FOR	INGREDIENTS TO AVOID
Dry skin	Heavier, oil-based moisturizer containing antioxidants, grape seed oil, or dimethicone, which help keep skin hydrated.	**Petrolatum:** Some moisturizers for excessively dry skin are petrolatum-based. Watch out for this ingredient because it can clog pores and disrupt body's natural ability to moisturize, leading to dryness and chapping. Manufacturers use it because it's really inexpensive.
Sensitive skin	Look for a glycerin-based moisturizer containing soothing ingredients such as chamomile or aloe.	**Alpha- and beta-hydroxy acids:** These may be good for acne and other skin types but can irritate sensitive skin and make it more sensitive to the sun. Also, watch out for potential allergens, such as fragrances or dyes.
Mature skin	Choose an oil-based moisturizer that contains the vitamin A compound retinol; copper peptides, which stimulate collagen production; and soy compounds, which build collagen fibers.	**Mineral oil:** This may also be listed as liquid paraffin or paraffin wax. It can clog pores or hinder your skin's natural ability to eliminate toxins. It can also be irritating with extended use.

As you may have figured out by now, I'm truly cuckoo for coconuts! Not only does coconut water hydrate you when you sip it, but this tropical H_2O hydrates your skin when you soak in it thanks to its cytokinins, which are a type of phytohormone. But all you really need to know is that it can help your skin replace damaged skin cells, improve circulation, and give you a lovely glow.

If you have dry skin, do this every day. It takes so little of the miraculous water to work, and when you compare it to high-end toners and moisturizers, it's cheaper than cheap!

WHAT YOU DO

Simply soak the cotton pads in coconut water, and then place them on your clean face. You'll probably need to lie down so they stay stuck to your skin and fully soak in. Keep them on for 10 to 15 minutes.

Skin Treatment #9:
Cooling Moisture Emulsion

WHAT YOU NEED

2 teaspoons coconut oil

1/2 cup heavy cream

This hydrating elixir is great to use at night before you go to bed. Coconut oil, with its saturated fat, vitamin E, and vitamin K, fights dryness and helps prevent wrinkles! Cream boasts lactic acid, which also helps anti-age your gorgeous skin. Plus, it cools and calms dry, irritated skin. Enjoy!

WHAT YOU DO

First, perform my *Ooh-La-La Lavender Pore Cleanser* to open your pores and start the deep moisturizing process. Then, thoroughly mix the coconut oil and heavy cream in a bowl. Apply it to your clean, damp skin in a circular motion. Let it set in for at five minutes. Use cool water to gently remove it. Don't use a washcloth or sponge to remove, because they can further irritate dry, flaky skin. Your skin will be left glowing and deeply moisturized.

Beyond these moisturizing treatments, I definitely recommend applying plenty of moisturizer (preferably with organic SPF) in the morning after you wash your face and again at night before you go to bed. Since you'll probably put on makeup in the morning, use a lighter moisturizer in the a.m. and a thicker one at night so your skin can soak in the hydro-goodness all night long. Always be gentle when you're applying moisturizer, and go in an upward motion instead of down—gravity does enough downward pulling, so we don't need to help it along.

At night, I love using just a little coconut oil on my skin. It really makes it soft and supple. I also sometimes use plain jojoba oil. Whatever you choose, the fewer ingredients listed on the bottle, the less likely the product is to irritate your skin or cause an allergic reaction.

Skin Snafu: Dull Skin

Do you ever wake up in the morning, trudge into the bathroom, and as you're brushing your teeth, you glance up, see yourself in the mirror, and think, "Where did my glow go?" It happens to me, too. Don't despair over dullness because there are remarkable, inexpensive ways you can get your glow on.

You can incorporate these in your overall plan just to maintain the beauty of your skin and help prevent it from aging.

Skin Treatment #10:
The Dull Skin Kiwi Remedy

WHAT YOU NEED

2 kiwis, pureed (can also use *substitutes*)

2 tablespoons plain yogurt

1 tablespoon orange juice

1 tablespoon olive oil

If I could hold one fruit above all the rest as a super fruit, it should be the kiwi. Full to the brim with beauty benefits like vitamin C and alpha-hydroxy fruit acids, this fuzzy phenomenon should grow with a medal on it.

WHAT YOU DO

Stir together all four ingredients and gently smooth it on your face and neck, avoiding the eye areas. Allow it to dry on your face, which will take around 15 minutes. Then, wash it off with warm water.

SUBSTITUTES: Other fruits that I (and your skin) adore and that brighten up dull, lackluster skin and give it an oh-so-glowing appearance are peaches, mangos, and papayas.

• • •

Gorgeous skin is always "in," and now you have some powerful tools for getting it. Soon, your friends will be asking how it's possible that you look like you just returned from a relaxing vacation...all thanks to your new, stunning glow. But more importantly, just imagine how Blissful you'll feel about yourself when you see soft, healthy, supple, youthful-looking skin when you look in the mirror. That's Blissfully beautiful you!

Chapter 4

Face Bliss

Now that you know all my secrets to skin Bliss, you might be wondering what to do about your lips, smile, and eyes. I knew it! Maybe I'm psychic. Or maybe I just know that the beauty of healthy, glowing skin can get lost if your teeth are dingy, your lips chapped and flaky, or the bags under your eyes are bigger than the one you carry your workout clothes in. So, let's fix all that, what do you say?

Put Your Best Face Forward

Your smile says so much about you. What better way is there to express your inner Bliss than through an ear-to-ear grin? But yellow teeth can get you down in the mouth and make you want to conceal your smile. According to one survey, 99.7 percent of adults said they think a smile is an important social asset (wouldn't you like to know what the other 0.3 percent were thinking?). And 96 percent believe a nice smile makes you more attractive to the opposite sex—not that you needed some study to prove that, but there are the cold, hard facts for you nonetheless. So, do you smile wide or tend to hide?

The pursuit of pearly whites can be an expensive one; in fact, on average, Americans empty $1.4 billion out of their wallets on over-the-counter teeth-bleaching products each year, according to the American Academy of Cosmetic Dentistry. That doesn't even include those super-pricey treatments you can have done only in the dentist's chair. Many of those bleaches can lead to some teeth and gum sensitivity—perhaps you've experienced it before—ouch! Well, open wide because I'm about to give you some less painful, more natural, and affordable methods to help you put on a happy face.

Teeth aren't the whole pretty picture, though! Think of your teeth as the painting and your lips as the frame—we all know how a bad frame can ruin a beautiful piece of art. If your lips are perpetually dry, chapped, and flaky, you've probably noticed how lipstick or gloss can cling onto the dry skin and leave your lips looking, well, yucky. We'll fix that problem faster than you can say, "Kiss me, darling!" Or maybe you find that your lips' natural hue is less than beautiful, even ghostly pale. You don't have to become addicted to your lipstick, ladies; there are natural and lasting ways to stain your lips and boost their natural color. *Voila*—your lips will soon be plump, lush, and divine!

When it comes to seeing someone's inner Bliss, the eyes have it, don't you think? The skin surrounding the eyes is so delicate and very sensitive to even minor changes in your body. Miss out on a couple hours of sleep, and I can guarantee it'll take extra concealer under your eyes to look even remotely normal. The same goes for when you're suffering with allergies or you're stressed out. The object is to detract from problems around your eyes so people will just focus on your bright, happy attitude shining through those peepers! I'll help you reduce puffiness and those obnoxious black circles without gobs of makeup.

So, come on, let's put your best face forward!

By the Skin of Your Teeth

Your teeth really do have skin on them, you know. Well, sort of. They have enamel. And that stuff is super strong, but it can get stained if you drink a lot of coffee, red wine, or acidic foods and drinks. Very acidic teeth-whitening products can, over time, weaken your tooth enamel, which you definitely don't want to do. This is why I prefer gentler methods.

Face Treatment #1:
Berry Brilliant Teeth Brightener

WHAT YOU NEED

1 to 2 large strawberries (washed and patted dry)

Whitening toothpaste

Strawberries have a couple of tricks up their tiny little sleeves to brighten up your teeth and remove stains. First, those seeds on their exterior act as mini teeth buffers when you rub them against the tooth surface. Also, strawberries have something called *malic acid*, which helps break down stains so they're more easily removed. The vitamin C in strawberries helps get rid of discoloration too. But remember what I said about acidic teeth-whitening products? The same applies here—you don't want to do this every day because it can end up hurting more than helping your enamel.

WHAT YOU DO

Cut the strawberry in half and gently rub the skin side along the surface of your teeth. Spend about 30 seconds on your top teeth and 30 seconds on your bottom teeth to give them a natural cleaning and stain removing. And then, brush your teeth with whitening toothpaste just to take it one step further into a total whiteout. Floss your teeth.

Now all that's left is to smile like you mean it...because you do!

Face Treatment #2:
Wipe Your Teeth Whiter

WHAT YOU NEED

Teeth wipes

Part of the reason your teeth can look dirty, yellow, and overall icky is thanks to a buildup of plaque and bacteria from the foods you're eating. A girl's gotta eat, and brushing your teeth multiple times a day is not only inconvenient, but it's unrealistic. Enter handy-dandy teeth wipes. A few companies make these cool products that usually just slip on your finger. You'll probably spot them in the dental hygiene aisle at your local grocery store.

WHAT YOU DO

Follow the instructions on the box, but I keep these with me and use them after a meal, a glass of wine, a cup of coffee, and so on, throughout the day. They can remove and prevent stains because they don't allow the food particles and acid to sit and marinate on your pearly whites all day long. Nifty, right?

Have It Made with Your Shade

While you're in the process of lightening and brightening up your chompers, choose a lipstick color that draws attention away from dingy teeth or stains. Your best bet is a lip gloss with a blue tinge or undertone instead of pink or nude colors, which can actually worsen the appearance of yellow teeth. If you choose red lipstick, pick one with a blue undertone to make your teeth shine even brighter and whiter.

Why Your Teeth Love Crunchy Munchies

Did you know that Mother Nature has provided us with toothbrushes in the form of certain foods? That's right, when you munch on raw, crunchy foods like apples, carrots, celeries, and the like, your teeth are being cleaned naturally. Stains can be lifted, and thus your teeth can appear lighter and brighter, thanks to the mild acids, astringents, and fiber in these foods. They also stimulate your salivary glands, and the extra saliva acts as an additional teeth and gum-cleaning fluid.

Not so into the crispy, crunchy snacks? Then reach for some yogurt or hard cheese. The experts think it might be the protein in these dairy foods that binds to the enamel, cleans them, and can even prevent cavities.

Got Thirsty Lips?

If your lips are chapped, flaky, irritated, or even itchy, they're probably parched and starved for moisture. Aside from feeling uncomfortable, your gloss or lipstick gets all clumpy and bumpy—the worst! Just like it's important to exfoliate the skin on your face and slough off the outer layers of skin, you need to buff up your lips too. It might seem counter-intuitive to use anything even slightly abrasive on irritated lips. But is coating on all those layers of lip balm doing you any good? Don't think so. For your lip moisture products to work, you have to first remove those flakes of dead skin.

Face Treatment #3:
World's Sweetest Lip Fix

WHAT YOU NEED

1 teaspoon brown sugar

1 teaspoon olive oil

Brown sugar acts as a wonderful, natural (and sweet!) exfoliant for your lips. It will encourage the top layer of dry skin to flake right off, and oil, with its vitamin E and healthy fats, will instantly hydrate the fresh, new lip skin.

WHAT YOU DO
Mix the sugar and olive oil together in a small bowl with your finger. Then, rub around your dry, lipstick-free lips for 30 seconds. Rinse it off with warm water, and you may need to use a gentle sponge or wash cloth to get the oil off completely. Follow up with a little lip balm or even a tiny dab of coconut oil. Yum!

Lips, I'm Here to Plump You Up

Wishing you had Scarlett Johansson-style lips? You and me both, darling! If you're not as well-endowed in the lip department as you'd like and the thought of visiting a plastic surgeon for a little filler nauseates either you or your bank account, all is not lost. Let's plump those lips to the point of luscious...no needles required!

Face Treatment #4:
Slim to Swell Lip Tonic

WHAT YOU NEED

1 teaspoon coconut oil

1/8 teaspoon ground cinnamon

2 drops peppermint essential oil

1 tube or small jar of lip balm

This little lip concoction gives your lips a nice plump, pouty look, thanks to the stimulating effects of these ingredients. The result isn't permanent, but it sure makes for a nice look for a photo session or an evening out!

Dry Lips, Empty Water Glass?

What happens if you don't water your flowers? They wilt and dry out. Well, if your lips are forever chapped, you might not be drinking enough water. Try doubling your water intake over the next 48 hours and see whether your lips perk back up.

WHAT YOU DO

Mix all the ingredients together in a small bowl. Use a cotton swab to dab on your lips. It might sting a little, especially if your lips are dry.

NOTE: You can also dab a little cinnamon essential oil on your lips for instant plumping. Any lip products containing mint, wintergreen, menthol, ginger, or cinnamon will cause your lips to swell up a bit.

Lips Lacking Luster?

There's nothing worse than getting called into a last-minute meeting or unexpectedly running into someone at the grocery store and real-izing—shoot!—you don't have your lipstick. If you have naturally pale lips, you might get questions like, "Are you feeling OK?" or "Hey, lady, do you need some oxygen?" Well, I hope it's not that bad. Fear not because nature, in all its wisdom, provided us with natural lip stains that can actually outlast your lipstick. True story!

Face Treatment #5:
You Can't "Beet" This Lip Stain

WHAT YOU NEED

Half a beet, chopped

1 tube or jar colorless lip balm

If you've ever cut into a beet, you've probably noticed its deep, rich colored juices can get everywhere. And maybe you've noticed that it's not that easy to wash off your hands. Great news: It works wonders on your lips! Especially if you want to give yourself a break from chemicals that might be in your makeup or lipstick, this is a great alternative.

WHAT YOU DO

Boil the chopped beet until soft, and then puree it in a blender or food processor. Mix a dab of the beets with a dab of the lip balm, and use a cotton swab to apply to lips. Just don't get any on your bright, white teeth!

Puffy Eyes Making You Cry?

Puffed-out eyelids and under-eye area can sure make it look like you've been crying or partying all night long! Ladies, as we get older, gravity and lack of elasticity work a number on the delicate skin around our eyes, and the end result is often that telltale puffiness we loathe.

Face Treatment #6:
The Milky Way to Keep Puff Away

WHAT YOU NEED

2 tablespoons cold milk

2 cotton balls

The lactic acid and essential nutrients like calcium in milk soothe and rejuvenate the skin around your eyes, and the coolness brings down swelling and will have you looking alert and happy as can be in no time.

WHAT YOU DO

Dip the cotton balls in the milk and give them a good squeeze so they're not sopping wet, but make sure they're very damp. Lie on your back, close your eyes, and gently set the cotton balls over your eyes. Stay put for ten minutes, and then remove the cotton balls; prepare to be amazed before you take a look in the mirror. Now you're ready to face the day.

Is It Salt's Fault?

Have you ever noticed how after a particularly sodium-laden meal your rings won't fit quite right, or maybe at all? All that salt can cause you to retain water, and guess what else that affects? Yes, it can make your eyes puffy. Beware of salt when you're eating out at restaurants especially. If you have an event, date, reunion, or wedding coming up, be sure to drink plenty of water and munch on fruits and veggies high in water (such as cucumbers and watermelon), and you'll quickly notice a difference in the area around your eyes.

My, My, What Dark Circles Under Eye

Dark circles under the eyes can have many causes from illness to allergies to lack of sleep to downright exhaustion. While you work out the root of the issue, here's a fix that can reduce the appearance of those dark half-moons under your lively eyes.

Face Treatment #7:
Smell the Rose, See the Results

WHAT YOU NEED

1 bottle rosewater

2 cotton balls

Rosewater is calming, cooling, and surprisingly effective at bringing your natural skin tone back to life and reducing the dark appearance of under eye bags because of its vitamin C.

WHAT YOU DO

You can get rosewater at most drug stores or health food stores. Its scent should bring to mind a lush rose garden—very relaxing. Soak two cotton balls in the water, and remove the excess. Lie on your back, close your eyes, and place the cotton balls on your eyes, making sure they're covering your black circles. Leave for 10 to 15 minutes, and then remove.

. . .

You can tell a lot about a person by their smile, can't you? If you're shining on the inside, that light will burn brightly on the outside too. And the reverse is true! It all goes back to Chapter 2, "Inner Bliss." Even the most glamorous and gorgeous of smiles can still convey a feeling of sadness or emptiness if that's what's brewing underneath. The key is to find your Bliss balance. Work on the exterior by whitening your teeth, plumping your lips, and depuffing your eyes while you're being good to yourself emotionally. Then, you'll surely take the breath of those whom you bestow your beautiful smile upon.

Chapter 5

Hair Bliss

Bad hair has the potential to set off your entire day on the wrong course. All because of your hair! It's crazy but true, don't you agree? As a matter of fact, a recent poll by ShopSmart, a *Consumer Reports* magazine, shows that 44 percent of women say that their mood is affected when they have a bad-hair day, and 26 percent have cried about their haircut. I mean think about it: Your hair can make you or break you. Just think about what it did for Jennifer Aniston (the "Rachel" cut), Farrah Fawcett, Meg Ryan, Rihanna, and Halle Berry, just to name a few. It can set you apart, and the $61-billion hair industry is proof. Think of how important a woman's hair is to her image, career, and sexuality. It's called our "crowning glory" for a reason. But there are some days when it's just a big, fat, frizzed-out mess on top of your head, and that can suck your Bliss dry. And did you know that the average woman spends $50,000 over her lifetime on her hair?!

I know it's sort of vain of us to invest so much emotion, effort, and money into the hair sprouting from our scalp, but we are women, and our hair matters, which is precisely why this entire chapter is devoted to your Hair Bliss!

Confession: I've had a couple rough hair days myself. One in particular. As you might imagine, my version of a hair blooper is actually closer to a hair catastrophe. It was the day before I was set to appear on *Good Day LA*, a morning news show in Los Angeles, so I wanted to get a little color refresher beforehand. It was supposed to be no big deal, just a few extra highlights. But I was feeling a little spontaneous, so when my eyes fell on a photo of Heather Locklear in a magazine while I waited, I thought—why not shake it up? "Let's go with this color," I exclaimed to my hairdresser as I pointed to the picture.

Before I tell you the rest of the story, I'd like to point out that this is a perfect example of me forgetting a basic Bliss principle: Set realistic goals. No matter how much my hairdresser of a dozen years tried to explain that I had a tinge of red in my hair and that Heather Locklear's color just wouldn't work on me, I was adamant. With eyes closed in indignation, I was shaking my head, not hearing a word of her pleading. I wanted her color, and I wasn't changing my mind.

Mixing hair dye is a skill that falls somewhere between chemist, artist, and wizard. It takes serious know-how, concentration, and sometimes a little luck. It was a particularly hectic day in the salon, and rather than mixing a pinhead of purple dye to take out the dullness in my hair, a frazzled assistant mistakenly poured in a dime-size portion. Maybe this difference in size doesn't seem dramatic—but just imagine using 1 cup of baking soda in a cookie recipe instead of 1/4 teaspoon. You couldn't cut those cookies with a chainsaw, much less eat them! Well, when they spun me around to face the mirror after washing my hair and that towel came off, I swear I heard the record scratch as everyone in the salon fell silent. My hair was purple. As in the color of Barney. The dinosaur.

Suddenly I was the most popular client in the joint. I had the attention of every colorist and stylist, all shaking their heads and mixing up plastic bowls of peroxide, dye, neutralizer, corrector, and whatever else they had in their arsenal to come to my rescue. Before I knew it, my scalp was covered in scabs from the harsh products, and I think I even saw a clump of my hair fall right out. Are you feeling my pain, you guys? Just as the team was about to throw in the towel, I remembered one of my very own tips—use whole milk to calm down burned-out and damaged hair shafts. It had worked for me, though not in situations quite this dire. I guess it was time to put my advice to the ultimate test. The assistant raced next door to the sandwich shop and bought a gallon of whole milk. Willing to try anything at this point, my hairdresser dumped it on my head and massaged it in. Instantaneously, my abused scalp felt relief. The lactic acid in the milk also soothed my strands so my hair was more able to absorb the final rinse they used to try to get it back to my hair color, or at least not make me look like I was dressed for Halloween in the middle of spring. Sure enough, it worked.

I walked out of that salon looking nothing like Heather Locklear but like the most beautiful version of myself. Now, let me return the favor by sharing some knockout hair info sure to tame your mane and banish those bad-hair days for good!

Getting to the "Root" of Your Hair

Did you know that you have between 100,000 and 150,000 hairs on your head? And don't panic if you notice many of them in the shower drain because we lose 50 to 100 hairs each day, on average. And if you have an "I'm so sick of my hair I just want to shave it all off" moment à la Britney Spears (which I don't recommend), it will likely grow back at the rate of about a half-inch per month. Sadly, as we get older, ladies, our hair is more susceptible to breakage. And it might get a little thinner. Or you may even start losing more hair. But don't shoot the messenger because then I couldn't tell you how to protect those lovely locks, no matter your age! Grab your round brush and blow-dryer, because you'll soon be having a love affair with your hair.

The Right Shampoo for Your Type

Every woman knows what she wants from her dream man. But do you know what you want and need from your shampoo? You should!

HAIR TYPE	WHAT TO LOOK FOR	WHAT TO AVOID
Oily hair	Natural astringents such as tea tree oil, sage, citrus oil, rosemary, stinging nettle, or chamomile will help reduce oil in the follicle. Clear shampoos are often a better choice than cloudy ones because they don't have as much conditioner that can weigh your hair down and leave a greasy residue.	It may seem counterintuitive, but avoid shampooing on a daily basis, because drying out your scalp can trigger an increase in oil production. Shampoo your hair two to three times per week. *Tip*: If you work out or get sweaty, just rinse it with water instead of doing a full wash.
Fine hair	Pick products with silicone, such as dimethicone or cyclomethicon, because they coat your strands with a thin film, creating fuller hair but without appearing wet or greasy. The silicone stays put even after you rinse.	Many volume-building hair products contain paraffin (beeswax), which builds up and can cause hair to break easier. Also avoid sodium lauryl/laureth sulfate, one the most common ingredients used in shampoo. Overuse can ultimately thin out your hair follicles because of its acidity.
Dry/damaged hair	Look for conditioners that have nut oils, shea butter, and wheat germ because they can bond to parched strands and improve the appearance of split ends.	Shampooing too often and harsh shampoos will only further damage and dry out your hair. If possible, find an alcohol-free shampoo; even consider a high-quality baby shampoo.

Your Hair Needs Some Love

Even if your hair already looks like it should be in a shampoo commercial, it still needs to be loved, and my favorite way to show my hair that I care is with argan oil. This miraculous oil is made from the nuts of the argan tree, which grows in Morocco. It's naturally high in vitamin E and antioxidants, which have restorative powers for hair that has been blown out, teased, curled, straightened, and styled to death for years. Just a few drops can show instant results—you'll notice your hair will be shinier and stronger, and you'll likely see fewer split ends because the oil hydrates and smooths the hair shafts. You can purchase it at most beauty-supply stores, but check the label and make sure it's imported from Morocco and made at an argan oil cooperative; otherwise, it may not be authentic. I recommend using it three times a week, or more if you wash and dry your hair daily. It's best to apply it to your hair right after washing and toweling dry. Rub two drops of the argan oil together in your palms, and then massage it through your hair, starting at the ends. Comb it through, and then dry and style as usual. I think if I was stranded on a desert island and I could take only a few items, argan oil would be one of them. It's that good, dolls!

The Once-a-Month Hair Bliss Boost

WHAT YOU NEED

1 jar of hair fertilizer (or root stimulator)

Quarter-size dollop of argan oil

This treatment works on any hair type, and I think it's smart to do once a month to maintain healthy, shiny hair. If your hair is particularly dry or frizzy, you can do this as often as twice a month but not more often since it can start to build up a bit. Hair fertilizer is a product that you can find at most drug stores. It's also often called a *root stimulator*. Look for ingredients like nettle and paprika, which are both natural herbs that will wake up the roots of your hair and encourage growth (but also beware of potential allergies). It's good on its own, but I find mixing it with argan oil in this treatment takes your hair to a whole new level of fabulous while taming the frizz and moisturizing your hair.

WHAT YOU DO

Do this procedure while your hair is dry. Massage just a small amount of the hair fertilizer into your scalp (read the instructions on the bottle) so that it gets right into the roots. Leave it on while you take the argan oil, and rub it into the ends of your hair because they need the most moisture. Leave in the products, gently pull your hair into a bun, and put on a shower cap for 15 minutes. Wash it out with a conditioning shampoo.

Frizzy Hair Love Affair

If you have just enough natural curl in your hair that it becomes a total frizz ball if the humidity gets above 1 percent, you know that styling your hair first thing in the morning is often a useless exercise. It's just going to do its own thing later anyway. Well, I'm coming to your rescue with hair treatments designed just for you.

Hair Treatment #1:
Vita-Avo-Coco Mask

WHAT YOU NEED

1 capsule vitamin E

2 tablespoons coconut milk

Half a ripe avocado, mashed

1 medium-sized bowl

The ingredients in this fantastic defrizzing hair mask contain essential vitamins and natural fats, which help plump and smooth out your strands. (By the way, eating these foods helps, too—remember, beauty comes from the inside out.)

Vitamin E protects your hair from the attack of free radicals, which you're exposed to all the time through pollution. The coconut milk is extremely moisturizing thanks to its high saturated fat content. Avocados also have natural fats, but they even have protein that will bind to your hair shaft and prevent frizz.

WHAT YOU DO

Mix together the avocado and coconut milk in a food processor or blender. Poke the vitamin E capsule with a safety pin, and squeeze the contents into the mixture. Stir it all together and massage it in, starting at the ends of your dry hair. Make sure every bit of your hair gets some of the treatment (depending on your length, you may need to make more). Gently pull your hair into a bun, and put on a shower cap for 20 minutes. Wash it out with a conditioning shampoo, and be sure to rinse it completely so your hair doesn't feel greasy later. If your hair is naturally oily, apply the mask about an inch below the roots so you don't stimulate excess oil production in the scalp.

Dull Hair Love Affair

Dull hair happens to everyone, regardless of color, type, or texture, and it is often caused by buildup of products, pollutants, and maybe even lack of attention. So, my dull hair treatments focus on stripping it of the buildup and rejuvenating your strands.

Hair Treatment #2:
Ultimate Brightening Rinse

WHAT YOU NEED

Your regular shampoo

1 teaspoon baking soda

Baking soda is great for cleaning your counters, but believe it or not, it also cleanses and purifies your hair. This is a simple fix you can do once a week, especially if you use a lot of hair products on a regular basis. Plus, it helps those products penetrate deeper into your hair!

WHAT YOU DO
In the shower, put some shampoo in your hair and lather it up. Before rinsing, add in the baking soda and thoroughly massage throughout your hair. Leave in for two minutes, and then rinse it all out and condition as usual.

Hair Treatment #3:
Banana Cream Hair Dream

WHAT YOU NEED
2 bananas

3 tablespoons mayonnaise

Several drops of argan oil

Your wildest hair dreams can come true, and you'll smell like a banana cream pie when you do this super-moisturizing hair treatment. Bananas are rich in potassium, which will give your hair a silky sheen. Mayo has vinegar, which helps draw out impurities and gets rid of buildup (just like the baking soda). Other ingredients in mayonnaise are eggs, lemon juice, and oil, all of which help boost your shine factor.

WHAT YOU DO
Put the bananas in a blender or food processor along with the mayonnaise and a few drops of argan oil. Once the mixture is smooth, apply it to dry hair, cover with shower cap, and leave on for 30 minutes. Shampoo out in the shower, and condition as usual.

Flat Hair Love Affair

Does your hair feel stuck to your head, stringy, flat, and lifeless? Step away from the teasing comb—let's pump up the volume and breathe some new life into your tresses without having to rat it to death.

Hair Treatment #4:
Yummy Honey Volumizer

WHAT YOU NEED

¼ cup honey

One 6-ounce container Greek yogurt (made with whole milk)

Small bowl

You may feel like you're baking a cake, but the sweet ingredients in this treatment go a long way toward taking your hair from flat to fab. Honey has antimicrobial properties and will actually help clean off the layers of grime from your hair while simultaneously infusing it with healthy moisture. Greek yogurt is high in calcium, protein, and the very same lactic acid that helped save my hair from a life of being purple! Together, this can be a powerful duo for plumping up your flat hair.

WHAT YOU DO

If you have shorter hair, you'll probably need only half the amount of these ingredients. In a small bowl, whip together the yogurt with the honey. If they're not incorporating well, add a little argan oil or olive oil to the mixture to help the honey liquefy. Spread it on your hair, starting at the ends and working your way up to the roots. Cover with a shower cap, and leave for 20 minutes. Then thoroughly wash out with your normal shampoo.

Fine Hair Love Affair

If your hair is super fine and appears thin, you need to thicken up those strands! Fine hair is more susceptible to damage, so it's important that you let your hair "rest" occasionally from the curling iron, flat iron, or blow dryer. And use this thickening treatment to fatten up your mane.

Hair Treatment #5:
Thickening Vitamin Hair Infusion

WHAT YOU NEED

Prenatal vitamins in liquid form

Prenatal vitamins truly offer the mother lode (ha!) of all essential nutrients, and while you probably think they can work their magic only if you swallow them, the truth is, your hair can absorb them, too. The high levels of vitamin D in these vitamins designed for moms-to-be will especially improve the health and vitality of your hair.

WHAT YOU DO

In the shower, first wet your hair, and then put one dose of the prenatal vitamin liquid in your hands. Rub it throughout your wet hair, and then let it set for five minutes before rinsing it out. Follow with your normal shampoo and conditioning routine.

NOTE: If the smell of the vitamins is too unpleasant, mix it with one drop of lavender essential oil.

Blow Dryer Meets (Leg) Hair

Your hairdryer has a whole new use, and it's not for the hair on your head! You want to keep your razor clean, safe, and bacteria-free, right? Well, if you just leave it in the shower after shaving, your razor stays moist and is more likely to rust and grow bacteria, making your next shave potentially dangerous! So, after you shave, give your razor a quick dry with the hairdryer. It takes only a few seconds to thoroughly dry it, and the added benefit is that this makes your razors last longer, saving you money! Get your dry on!

· · ·

The good news is you really can improve the condition of your hair so you aren't haunted by bad-hair days anymore. But try to be realistic. If you're striving to have hair like what you see in fashion magazines, you're probably deluding yourself. Come on, no one's hair actually looks like that! But if you spend some extra time giving TLC to your strands, they'll repay you by looking thicker and shinier and behaving better in general. Dare to have prettier hair!

Chapter 6

Nails Bliss

You might be wondering what pretty nails have to do with finding true Bliss in your life. Well, your eyes may be the window to your soul, but your hands and nails also tell a story about you. When you first meet someone, you greet them with a (firm) handshake, and many of us tend to talk with our hands. If your hands and nails are ragged, dry, and unkempt, you're sending a message to potential employers, partners, and other important folks you encounter—and that message isn't a good one. Plus, you can totally tell how old someone is just by looking at their hands. I'm always amazed when I meet someone who obviously spends a mint getting their face pulled, plucked, and plumped but they completely neglect their hands! If you're trying to maintain your overall youthful look, maintaining your hands, nails, and, yes, even your toenails, is all part of the deal. So, let's keep them all in tip-top shape—easily and cheaply!

You're Tough as Nails...

...but are your nails as strong as they could be? Your nails are made up of layers of a substance called *keratin*, which is a type of protein. The healthiest nails are smooth, strong ones. If you have pits, ripples, ridges, grooves, or spots, your nails aren't Blissful...and neither are you when you look down at them! Perhaps you've been hiding them under gels or acrylics for years so you're not exactly sure about the current state of your actual nails. You don't have to soak them all off to find out—just check your tootsies and see how your toenails are doing. It's smart to know what's going on with your nails, because they can actually be an indicator of vitamin deficiencies or other health problems.

Women, maybe more than ever, are hyper-aware of the appearance of our nails. In the last year, we purchased 50 percent more nail polish and nail-care services than the year before. Wow! But here's a fact that just took the cake for me—did you know there's a manicure that costs $51,000? Yes, you saw three zeros! It includes the application of ten carats of diamonds directly to your nails. (Imagine how horrified you'd be if you chipped one and left a diamond behind somewhere?) Stick with me, and I'll show you how to beautify your nails for a little less than a down payment on a home. Ha!

Putting just a little time into taking care of your nails will reap you big rewards. I'm a fan of the occasional spa-style mani-pedi as a form of relaxation or even celebration (like a mommy-daughter day together), but if the owner of the nail salon calls to see whether you're alive when you miss your weekly appointment, please allow me to save you some serious cash with some simple, at-home nail techniques. These work so well that it'll look like you should quit your day job and model engagement rings full-time. (Yup, that's a real job! But I digress.)

Cuter Cuticles

What's worse than a hangnail? OK, maybe a paper cut. All right, there are a lot of things worse than a hangnail in life, but still, they're not fun in the least. They are, however, fully avoidable, simply by taking proper care of your cuticles. It's better not to cut them because they can grow back unevenly, and if you cut too far, you leave yourself vulnerable to infection. Give these at-home techniques a whirl instead.

Nail Treatment #1:
Ultimate Ragged Cuticle Cure

WHAT YOU NEED

1 teaspoon baking soda

1/2 cup warm water

2 teaspoons fresh lemon juice

1 teaspoon honey

1 teaspoon coconut oil

1 cuticle stick

Baking soda is a nonabrasive cleanser that can buff your nails and cuticles. Honey penetrates your cuticles, giving them healthy, natural moisture so they don't get ragged. The honey also kills any bacteria your nails may be harboring. The acidity of the lemon juice helps slough off dead skin cells.

WHAT YOU DO

First, use just a couple drops of water to turn the baking soda into a paste. Rub the paste around on the cuticles of your clean, unpolished nails. Then, mix together the lemon juice and honey. Combine the mixture with the warm water in a small bowl. Dip your fingertips, with the baking soda paste on them, into the mixture and let them soak for five minutes. Rinse in warm water, and then pat dry. Rub a tiny bit of coconut oil into the cuticles, and then use the cuticle stick to push the cuticles back. Don't push down too hard on the nail as you go. Lastly, rinse and towel off the coconut oil. Ta-da! You now have clean, even cuticles.

Nail Treatment #2:
Dry Cuticle Renewal

WHAT YOU NEED

1 egg yolk

5 tablespoons pineapple juice

You probably wouldn't think to put pineapple juice in your omelet, but the combo is great...when you soak your nails in it. Pineapples have an enzyme called *bromelain*, which has natural anti-inflammatory properties. In this case, it helps soften and treat the dry skin and cuticles surrounding your nails. Egg yolks, with their fatty acids and protein, moisturize and further heal the area around your nails.

WHAT YOU DO
Stir together the egg yolk and pineapple juice in a small bowl. Soak your nails in the mixture for five minutes, and then use a cotton swab to push the cuticles back. Rinse well and pat dry.

Achy, Breaky Nails?

If your nails are brittle and break or chip easily, they might be lacking moisture. (There are other causes like aging and even certain medical conditions, so if you're concerned, you may want to show your doc at your next physical.) Since nails don't naturally have any fat, they're unable to retain moisture of any kind. Lend them a helping hand with these moisture methods.

Nail Treatment #3:
Strong As Nails Weekly Soak

WHAT YOU NEED

1/3 cup vegetable oil (or you can use pretty much any oil you have in your cupboard like olive, coconut, avocado, walnut, or macadamia oil)

What Goes In Will Grow Out

Longing for stronger, healthier nails? Munch on some cauliflower with your next salad or steam it up as a side dish. Cauliflower provides biotin, a nutrient vital to nail health, growth, and strength.

Especially if your hands are in and out of water a lot, your nails can dry out and become brittle. Natural, fragrance-free oils are easier for your nails and the skin around them to absorb than regular lotion or hand cream.

WHAT YOU DO
Put the oil into a small bowl, and soak your unpolished nails in it for five minutes. You can also do this for your toenails, but you'll probably need a bigger bowl and a bit more oil. An alternative is just to rub a tiny bit of oil into each nail and let it soak in for a few minutes before washing your hands.

Nail Treatment #4:
Strong Nails, Extra Garlic

WHAT YOU NEED

1 clove fresh garlic

1 bottle clear nail polish

You'll probably feel a little silly, and you'll definitely smell like an Italian food restaurant, but I'm telling you, this works! Garlic is a nutritional powerhouse, with its calcium, iron, and B vitamins, all of which happen to be key ingredients to strong, healthy nails.

WHAT YOU DO
Mince up the garlic clove into tiny pieces that will fit into the bottle of nail polish. I like using a bottle of polish that is partially used so there's

plenty of room for the minced garlic. Add the garlic to the polish, and then let it marinate for 7 to 10 days. Just like when you infuse oil with garlic, it takes time for it to really combine. Once it's been at least a week, paint your clean, unpolished nails with the garlic-infused polish. For best results, apply the polish once a week for about a month.

Mellow Your Yellow

Yellow roses are pretty. Yellow nails are not (just like yellow teeth as we've already discussed). A yellowing of the nails can occur for many reasons. I've always noticed my nails tend to get stained yellow after I wear dark nail polish for a long period of time, but it can also mean you've got an oh-so-dreaded nail fungus. (Just the word *fungus* is kinda creepy, don't you agree?) I sincerely hope you never have a brush with this annoying affliction, but in case you do, you'll find some remedies here.

Nail Treatment #5:
Effervescent Nail Whitener

WHAT YOU NEED

Denture-cleaning tablets

Water

Did you ever imagine that there could be a use for denture cleaner other than cleaning dentures? Well, those magical tablets are great for bringing your nails back to their clean, natural state too. Give them a good soak and see for yourself.

WHAT YOU DO

Dissolve the denture cleaner in a bowl of water, and soak your nails in the liquid. Watch the yellow fade away! (It may take a couple of treatments.)

Nail Treatment #6:
Fungus Among Us Fix

WHAT YOU NEED

1 bottle tea tree oil

1 cup apple cider vinegar

Water

Patience is the key when it comes to nail fungus. You want to kill the fungus and then let the affected nail grow off. The acid from the apple cider vinegar makes it harder for the fungus to survive. And the tea tree oil helps restore the natural appearance of the nails. Keep taking your vitamins and supplements so your nails grow faster, and the fungus grows right off. I know it's no fun to wait this long for it to go away, but it sure beats taking some of the serious medications doctors prescribe to fight the fungus!

WHAT YOU DO

For toenail or fingernail fungus infections, mix one part vinegar and two parts warm water, and soak your nails for 15 to 20 minutes per day for six months. Then, apply tea tree oil directly to all of your nails twice daily. Just put a drop on every nail and let it soak in.

Outsmart Your Ingrowns!

You can ease ingrown toenail pain with a 20-minute warm Epsom salt soak. A temporary fix when it's throbbing is to put just a dab of over-the-counter tooth or gum pain reliever directly on the affected toenail. It'll numb it right up.

I know, I know, it feels like there aren't enough hours in the day to even think about spending time beautifying your nails. But I want to encourage you to slow down, take a breath, and realize that you deserve a little "you" time. Even if you have to schedule a nail appointment with yourself to fit it in, so be it. When you look down at your healthy, shiny nails while you're driving, typing, or changing a diaper, you'll be glad you made the effort. On the other hand, if you're a once-a-week nail salon type of girl, the methods in this chapter are great ways to extend the time between your appointments to save money, and they're also healthier than harsh chemicals you might encounter at the local nail place. Hands down, it's a Blissful win-win.

Chapter 7

Body Bliss

Feeling Blissful about your body is no small feat. There's a lot of pressure on us to have it all: the ideal marriage, a picturesque home, amazing careers, plenty of income, successful children, fabulous clothes, and, of course, a gorgeous body to show them off. One of those plates we're furiously spinning is destined to come smashing down—and, inevitably, the first to go is often the body plate (excuse the pun). We sacrifice the time it takes to make a healthy breakfast so we can use that time to focus on the kids, the husband, or the gazillion other people and things that demand our attention. Or we can't carve out a 45-minute work-out because there just aren't enough hours in the day. We push ourselves, our health, and our bodies to the side to make way for everything and everyone else we're managing.

Body Bliss only partially refers to what you see in the three-way mirror when you try on bathing suits at the mall. It's about constantly doing simple things that will help you love how you look and feel so that when you walk into a PTA meeting, your high-school reunion, a job interview, or even the grocery store, you look your best and you know it. In this chapter, I'm going to show you exactly what to eat and do to help you reach your Body Bliss goal and stay there. I'm talking about all the ingredients you put in your body that can help you look and feel better. I'm not a nutritionist, but I have a food formula that can change your body and your attitude. You'll also learn how you can implement easy ways to burn calories every day that won't feel anything like exercise. I've learned so many tricks from supermodels and actresses I've interviewed over the years that I will share with you. One actress told me that every time she stayed at a hotel, she requested her room to be on a very high floor so she could take the stairs every single time she went to her room. She'd just pop off those Louboutins and carry them as she raced up flight after flight in that stairwell. Now that's dedication, but it's also doable for everyone no matter how busy you are.

Can we just keep this next part between us? Shhhh—I don't want to get blackballed. There's a conspiracy against me in Hollywood as evidenced by the fact that high-definition TV "coincidentally" (wink) came out the day I turned 40. You know: HDTV is what magnifies every line, freckle, or discoloration and every extra pound a hundred times over for the world to see! Uggh. Happy flippin' birthday to me! Back in the days of Grace Kelly, they would enhance her beauty by smearing Vaseline on the camera lens or choosing special lighting. But ohhh nooo...now the goal is to make viewers feel like they're practically inside the studio, so the camera crews use bright lights and magnifying camera lenses and technology that accentuates reality with all its flaws. Since I've chosen this career path and to be on the screen, I have to do what I can to look my best, especially in high-def.

I admit: I'm very susceptible to fad diets. I've tried a cabbage diet, a pineapple diet, a tomato-only diet, and a myriad of others, but only one gave me quick results—though not exactly the kind I wanted.

I read in some gossip magazine that a big-time celebrity was having great success on a diet that consisted of only orange-colored foods. I was instantly intrigued and ran out to purchase bushels of carrots, tangerines, bell peppers, apricots, and the like. (Sadly, Cheetos weren't on the list.) It really didn't take long to notice a change in my appearance. No, I wasn't thinner. I was orange. Seriously, I would have fit in well at Willy Wonka's Chocolate Factory as one of the Oompa Loompas. Just imagine if this had been during my brief purple hair phase—can you say Teletubbie? Oy vey. But hey, I had near X-ray vision thanks to all the beta-carotene in the carrots, so at least I had that going for me!

Ultimately I recognized that following a celebrity's "alleged" diet plan was a bit absurd, so I gave it up, and my orange hue quickly dissipated. Most importantly, years later I have figured out what does work, and I can help you unlock the secrets too.

Foods That Boost Your Bliss

Most women I know have a complex relationship with food, thanks in part to all the information and misinformation floating around. We end up asking ourselves, "Is there trans-fat in this mac 'n' cheese? Will this energy bar increase my cortisol? Is this banana gonna spike my blood sugar?" We've probably all had thoughts along these lines, sometimes to the point that we'd rather just not eat at all than have to listen to our own onslaught of theories and second-guessing.

Have you ever gone on a starvation-style cleanse, an all-protein diet, or any other kind of extreme food plan? And did you notice that you felt, well, bad? Maybe you were tired, crabby, sad, or even angry? I'm no nutritionist, but I do understand that when your nutrition is unbalanced and you're not getting enough of the nutrients your body needs to function, you'll likely feel uncomfortable physical and emotional side effects. Thus, you couldn't possibly be anywhere near your most Blissful state on those types of restrictive food plans. Who could stick with a diet like that for more than a few days anyway? Not me, that's for sure!

Sometimes we turn to food when it seems like nothing and no one could ever ease our pain. Call it what you will: self-medicating, emotional eating, or soothing an aching heart by controlling what we put in our mouth. I've found that this potentially destructive habit can strike when we're stressed, bummed out, overtired, lonely, or scared—the list of causes is different for everyone, but I'm guessing you can relate. The instinct is to reach for comfort food such as cake, ice cream, French fries, or chocolate, but the temporary relief disappears as soon as the last bite hits our lips.

What if you could train yourself to crave foods that actually satisfy your physical and emotional hunger, without sacrificing your girly figure? I'm talking about foods that you can enjoy while simultaneously getting closer to your ultimate body goals. Enter Bliss foods. Studies show that certain foods can boost levels of chemicals linked to happiness in your brain. Here are my top 10 favorite recipes that use nature's magic ingredients to increase your Bliss.

Top Ten Bliss Foods List

Starting right now, Bliss Foods are your new comfort foods. You can munch on these guilt-free snacks that can actually make you feel better in the moment and beyond. They can help burn fat, nourish your body, and even give you healthier skin, hair, and nails. And they can turn bathing suit shopping into a less torturous experience no matter how bad the department store lighting is because you'll be closer to having the gorgeous body you've always wanted. Yes, I'm for real. These Body Bliss recipes will get your creative juices flowing and whet your appetite!

#1: Pineapple

This sweet, juicy, tropical wonder is loaded with fiber, which is great for digestion and naturally managing your weight. It also gives you a quick energy boost because of its natural sugars but without the crash.

Recipe Ideas

Pineapple tastes yummy chopped up and added to Greek yogurt, thrown into a smoothie, or even eaten by itself as a dessert.

#2: Tuna

It's a super-healthy fish that's naturally high in selenium, which is a key nutrient in regulating mood and anxiety. A low-fat, high-protein fish that could help keep the worry away? I say, yes, please!

Recipe Idea:
Easy-Peasy Tuna Wrap

WHAT YOU NEED

1 packet or can tuna packed in water

1 low-carb tortilla or wrap

Half of a green bell pepper

Quarter of an avocado, mashed

1 small handful sprouts

Half of a cucumber, thinly sliced

1 teaspoon Dijon or yellow mustard

1 to 2 large romaine lettuce leaves, shredded or torn

Salt and pepper to taste

Yield: 1 serving

WHAT YOU DO

Spread the mustard and avocado on the tortilla, and then add the tuna. Layer on the rest of the veggies in whichever order you like. Wrap it up and chow down!

#3: Sesame Seeds

These crunchy, delicious little seeds contain a certain amino acid called *threonine*. Studies have shown that people suffering with depression tend to have lower levels of this amino acid than people who aren't depressed. How about that?

Recipe Ideas

Sprinkle sesame seeds on top of a salad or stir them in your soup. They're also delicious on top of whole wheat toast and a little smear of almond butter. Yum!

#4: Grapefruit

Citrusy, juicy, tangy, and sometimes sweet, these delicious fruits are vitamin C powerhouses. It's been reported that vitamin C can help reduce feelings of stress or anxiety because it plays a role in normalizing your stress hormones. In case that's not enough motivation for you, there's a bonus: According to research, the scent of grapefruit can actually cause men to perceive some women as six years younger than their actual age. So, if you want to defy your age, dab a little grapefruit essential oil behind your ears.

Recipe Idea:
The Pink & Green Energy Machine

WHAT YOU NEED

Half of a grapefruit

4 leaves of fresh mint

1 tablespoon of organic liquid stevia

Yield: 1 serving

WHAT YOU DO

Whisk stevia and chopped mint together. Then, drizzle on top of the grapefruit that has been sectioned. Enjoy!

#5: Butternut Squash

A type of winter squash with orange, nutrient-dense flesh, this veggie is filled to the brim with zinc, which can stimulate your nerve cells, and some studies have indicated that it helps fight depression.

Recipe Idea:
The "I Can't Believe It's Butternut" Squash Bliss Dish

WHAT YOU NEED

1 butternut squash (peeled and cut into 1-inch chunks, seeds removed)

2 tablespoons crushed cashews

Nonstick spray

Salt and pepper to taste

Yield: 4 servings

WHAT YOU DO

Preheat the oven to 375 degrees. Once you've (carefully!) sliced the squash, spray lightly with cooking oil and sprinkle with salt and pepper. Bake on a baking sheet or casserole dish for 45 minutes or until soft. Turn the oven down to 200 degrees. Sprinkle the finely crushed cashews over the top of the squash, and bake for another five minutes. Eat and be Blissful!

#6: Salmon

This beautiful, pink fish is high in omega-3 fatty acids, which is fantastic for your brain's health. It can also stave off depression and improve mood.

Recipe Idea:
Bliss Salad with a Tropical Twist

WHAT YOU NEED

2 cups raw baby spinach

1 serving steamed or grilled salmon fillet, chopped into bite-size chunks

Half of a papaya, cut into 1/2-inch cubes

1 teaspoon sunflower seeds

1 tablespoon olive oil

Yield: 1 serving

WHAT YOU DO

You can buy a small, raw salmon filet and prepare it at home, or you can do what I prefer, which is to ask the seafood department at my grocery store to steam the fillet for me so I can just take it home, chop it up, and add it to my salad. Either way, place your cleaned baby spinach into a large salad bowl. Dump in the papaya, sunflower seeds, and salmon. Drizzle olive oil over the top. Feel Bliss as you chow down!

#7: Asparagus

This spear-like green vegetable features a type of B vitamin called *folic acid*, which can help your brain sustain healthy levels of serotonin, a feel-good chemical.

Recipe Ideas

Chop it up and throw it in a sauté pan along with some chicken, and then serve it over whole wheat pasta or quinoa.

#8: Dark Chocolate

Cacao is basically chocolate, in its most natural form. Dark chocolate made up of at least 70 percent cacao is the healthiest for you, and it can increase serotonin levels in the brain, which leads to happy feelings. This isn't permission to gorge yourself on dark chocolate bars! Just a little goes a long way.

Recipe Ideas

You can add an ounce of dark chocolate nibs to a protein shake, or just pop them in the microwave for a few seconds and dip strawberries in the melted deliciousness.

#9: Almonds

These nuts boast high levels of magnesium, which has been shown to help your brain manage stress and your body in its natural energy production. Almonds are also very filling—the perfect fix for an afternoon craving.

Recipe Ideas

Grab a handful of raw almonds as a snack, or try adding almond milk or almond butter to a smoothie. They're also delicious when slivered and added to green beans or any other steamed veggie.

#10: Broccoli

Did you have any idea that broccoli is high in calcium? Well, it's true. Calcium is great for protecting bone health, but researchers also say if you're low in calcium, you are more likely to be moody and experience nervousness because it's responsible for telling your body to release certain neurotransmitters that bring on general good feelings. Maybe broccoli isn't the first food you think of putting in a smoothie, but believe me, this is a delicious combination, and it will give you such a boost.

Recipe Idea:
The "Who Knew Broccoli Belonged in a Blender?" Smoothie

WHAT YOU NEED

1 fresh or frozen banana

1½ cup low-fat coconut milk (or low-fat vanilla almond milk)

1 handful fresh or frozen broccoli

1 teaspoon organic liquid stevia (or 1 tablespoon honey)

Juice of half a lemon

1 teaspoon cinnamon

Yield: 1 smoothie

WHAT YOU DO

First blend the coconut milk, lemon juice, organic stevia, banana, and cinnamon, preferably using a high-powered blender (but any blender will likely work). Then, add the broccoli and blend on high until it's smooth. It's broccoli Bliss with a straw.

Your Blissful Blender

Now that I've convinced you that broccoli can go in a blender, here's a trick that works with many vegetables. If you (or someone in your family, adult or pint-sized) aren't exactly the type to snack on celery and carrots or request steamed spinach instead of French fries, then allow me to introduce you to the wonders of your Blissful blender. Once you mix kale, spinach, lettuce, broccoli, or even carrots together with the sweet goodness of banana, berries, oranges, apples, kiwi, or any other yummy fruit you can dream of, your taste buds won't detect the veggie presence, but your body sure will. You might need to experiment with flavor combinations, but once you get it just right, you'll actually look forward to eating (well, drinking) your leafy greens. Herbs like mint or basil can taste delicious in these concoctions as well. Don't forget to raid the spice cabinet too—a dash of cinnamon, pumpkin pie spice, cloves, ginger, allspice, or nutmeg can really take smoothies to a whole new level of Bliss.

Foods That Diss Your Bliss

In order for good to exist, we've also got evil—I know, deep thoughts, right? But it's true, especially when it comes to foods that affect your Bliss. Just like all the foods and recipes in this chapter can help change your body for the better and put you in a more Blissful mood, there are foods that can make you feel lethargic, sad, and even cause your brain to shrink! For example, studies show that you're at higher risk of having depression if you're a fast-food addict who can't resist the dollar menu at the drive-thru. I can't think of anything more opposite of Bliss than depression, can you? I highly encourage you to avoid these foods, so let me get more specific.

"Debbie Downer" Foods

Fatty Foods: You know what I mean here: hamburgers, pizza, fast foods, and fried foods. Not only can they trigger a serious case of guilt, regret, and "why can't I button my pants?" syndrome, but there have even been studies showing that people who eat these foods regularly are 51 percent more likely to suffer with depression.

Sugary Foods: I'm not saying you can never indulge at the local cupcake shop again, but super-sweet foods give you a quick energy surge and then leave you hanging when you come down off the "high." So, you'll likely find yourself dragging around until you finally give in and take a nap. Maybe share your cupcake with a girlfriend on special occasions and replace an afternoon candy snack with any of the Bliss Foods.

Caffeine: What? Caffeine is a "downer?" Well, kind of. Too much of it can make you dehydrated, which can cause an overall feeling of sadness or fatigue. It can also really give you a case of the jitters. If you can't imagine what your morning would look like without a stop at the local Starbucks, try going decaf every other day or going with a small size instead of that venti. Another idea is to order your coffee as half-caffeinated, half-decaf.

Alcohol: You may have noticed that the good mood you get from a glass of wine is fleeting. Too much of it can mess up your blood sugar levels, cause dehydration, and even lead to anxiety and depression.

Rise 'n' Shine Minty Lime

WHAT YOU NEED
3 fresh mint leaves

Juice of half of a lime

8 ounces of pure water

I drink this every morning as soon as I wake up, and it gives me such a Blissful lift that I just have to share it with you. When you sleep, you're obviously not drinking any water, so when you wake up, it's really important to start rehydrating right away. It will perk you (and your tissues) up and give you energy to conquer the day. I add the lime to even further combat any lethargy with its vitamin C, and the mint fights that icky morning breath while also boosting my vitamin A. It's really the perfect combo.

WHAT YOU DO
Crush up the fresh mint leaves in the bottom of a glass like you're preparing a mojito. Then squeeze the fresh lime juice into a glass and pour in the pure water. Drink up!

Think Outside the Gym

A key aspect of achieving body Bliss is finding ways to incorporate exercise into your everyday life. This will not only improve your health but also whittle your middle, tone your muscles, and help you love what you see in the mirror, even when you're in the buff. You don't have to be chained to the treadmill or pay for expensive exercise classes. Sure, those are great ways to work out, and I'm not trash talking the gym or the booming fitness industry. I just know we're often way too busy to dedicate additional time for burning calories and breaking a sweat, so I have Blissful news for you. Exercise can happen anytime, anywhere at no cost. True!

Whenever you're schlepping around kids, groceries, or potting soil, you're burning calories, building muscle, and melting fat. Personally, I never stay put for one solid hour without getting up, dancing around, doing jumping jacks, taking a stroll around the block, or walking Tom Brady. (Not the real Tom Brady. That's our dog's name. I don't think the real one would appreciate the leash.)

You might think you know everything there is to know about getting fit. But I'm here to inspire and encourage you to get creative and find ways to make it painless and 100 percent doable, so here are a few ideas to get you going. I used a calorie counter and based it on a 150-pound woman, so it's not perfectly accurate for everyone, but it should give you a good idea of how many calories you can burn just adding a few simple moves to your daily routine. You don't have to stick strictly to these, though. Come up with your own list of fun, unique, and, preferably, silly ways to throw your weight around and torch some fat!

It goes without saying (but I'm saying it anyway!) that you should discuss any kind of new exercise routine or changes to your current habits with your doctor before you begin, especially if you have any health challenges. I may be an expert at what works for me, but I'm certainly not a substitute for all the lovely experts in your life. Got it? Good. Now for some fitness inspiration!

Bright Ideas for Bliss-ercise

ACTIVITY	AVERAGE CALORIES BURNED	OTHER BLISS BENEFITS
Outdoor yard work: prune, mow, weed whack, plant, or pot something! *(30 minutes)*	178 calories	Tightens core, increases vitamin D intake, tones arms and legs
Do lunges while vacuuming the floors. *(30 minutes)*	125 calories	Strengthens thighs, tones butt, improves balance
Wash your car. (And I don't mean drive it through the car wash! Think garden hose, bucket, and sponge.) *(30 minutes)*	107 calories	Full body workout, sculpts biceps, engages core, and strengthens leg muscles
Arm/back exercise with a broom! Hold broomstick to left side and lift right arm overhead. Lean left as you extend right leg to side. Lift right leg and lower. Do 10 times and switch sides. Then, sweep the floor. Repeat! *(20 minutes)*	80 calories	Improves posture, works out abs, tones arms, and improves balance
Walk your dog. (Or, better yet, jog your dog!) *(20 minutes)*	78 calories	Lowers blood pressure, manages weight, improves cholesterol
Wash dishes while doing calf raises. Calf raises: Point toes inward, push down through your toes, lifting heels off ground. Hold for 5 seconds and repeat at least 15 times. Then point toes outward and repeat set. Then face feet forward and repeat again. *(30 minutes)*	61 calories	Chisels calf muscles, tones arms

ACTIVITY	AVERAGE CALORIES BURNED	OTHER BLISS BENEFITS
Give your partner a back massage. (15 minutes)	71 calories	Tones arms and upper body/shoulder area, improves hand strength
Have a dance party in your living room! (This can be done solo or with a partner.) (10 minutes)	53 calories	Enhances flexibility, reduces stress, makes you smile/laugh, helps maintain weight, improves balance (May even improve your dance moves!)
Ditch the grocery cart—carry your groceries to the car (and park far away!). (7 minutes) Bonus: Do bicep curls with the bags!	35 calories (including the bicep curls)	Engages all muscles in body, strengthens biceps

More Blissful Calorie Burn Ideas

Now that I got started, I can't stop! Here are more ideas to get your creative juices—and body—flowing.

While watching TV: Stand up and do squats during commercial breaks.

While reading a book: Do wall sits for one-minute intervals.

Anywhere with stairs: Take the stairs instead of escalator or elevator—and go up and down several times instead of just getting to your destination.

While brushing teeth: Balance on one leg.

While cleaning the house: Walk around on your toes to sculpt your calves.

At home (or wherever you feel it's appropriate): Do the bunny hop! All that bouncing up and down is great, as long as your knees can take it.

While driving: Squeeze your butt cheeks. Work those glutes!

While at your desk (or anywhere): Engage your core by pulling your belly button toward your spine. Flex and sculpt those abs. (You don't have to do crunches in order to tone your tummy.)

All the time: Walk more! (*Bonus:* Buy a pedometer and see how many steps you take each day; 2,000 steps burn approximately 100 calories.)

Why 22 Minutes of Bliss-ercise?

You'll find in the Bliss Plan that I recommend incorporating 22 minutes of *Bliss-ercise* per day, six days per week. How did I come up with that magical number? There have been so many studies conducted around the world about the exercise "sweet spot," or the exact number of minutes per day that we need to get our heart rates up in order to stay healthy. Ultimately, they're all in the range of 20 to 30 minutes. Well, I'm not a fitness expert, but I do know what's realistic for busy women like me. I think 30 minutes seems daunting and 20 minutes seems like it's not even worth it, so in both cases, you probably won't commit. But 22 minutes feels just right (I'm like the Goldilocks of exercise), and if you do it six days a week, then you're likely taking care of your fitness requirements. Of course, if you want to and have time, aim for more! But 22 minutes is a length of time I think we can all live with, so go for it!

Sore Muscles from All That Movin' and Groovin'?

Now that you're basically going to be sculpting a beautiful bod all day, every day, you might notice a little bit of soreness. In my opinion, even the best massage can't compete with the medicinal effects of a nice, warm Epsom salt bath.

Body Bliss Treatment #1:
The Mystical, Magical Epsom Salt Bath

WHAT YOU NEED

2 to 3 cups Epsom salt (depending on size of your tub)

Bathtub with warm water

10 drops lavender essential oil

Maybe your grandma taught you this trick many years ago, and Grandma sure did know best. Everyone from models to marathon runners swear by an Epsom salt bath to help reduce swelling and soreness. The magnesium and sulfates in the Epsom salts help draw out toxins and even fade bruises. And it's just downright relaxing.

WHAT YOU DO

Pour the Epsom salt and essential oil under the warm running water, and make sure they dissolve in the bath water. (Ideally you can lock the door and not be disturbed by kids, the phone, and your beckoning to-do list.) Enjoy the bath for 20 to 30 minutes.

NOTE: You can purchase bags of Epsom salt for five or six dollars at your local pharmacy or grocery store.

Fun Facts from the Brainiacs

You can thank the small town of Epsom in England for its miraculous spring where the "salt" was first produced. I put "salt" in quotations because it's actually a misnomer—Epsom salt is a mineral compound made of magnesium, sulfur, and oxygen. And I usually have a couple bags of them under my bathroom sink right next to extra rolls of toilet paper because I really think both are essential!

Pre-Party Body Bliss

You've had it in your Outlook calendar for months, but just this Monday you realize that your cousin Mary is having her engagement party on the rooftop of a swanky hotel...on Saturday. And, of course, an ex-boyfriend you haven't seen in years will be in attendance. Perfect, right? You've been stressed out, worn out, and fresh out of energy to work out, so your body is far from Blissful (or from fitting in that dress you'd hoped to wear). All is not lost, so perk up and read on. Here are some of the top tricks even Hollywood glamour girls employ when getting red-carpet ready.

Body Bliss Treatment #1:
The Incredible Shrinking Woman Wrap

WHAT YOU NEED

10 rolls of medical bandages

1 roll plastic wrap

1 cup Epsom salts

1 cup sea salt

1 cup baking soda

3 cups very warm water

Optional: 5 drops essential oil of your choosing (to add lovely scent)

Sure, I got a lot of laughs and looked pretty silly when I did this body wrap on Ellen, but I'm telling you, it tightens up the jiggle in a jiffy! And if I can do it on national television, you can do it in the privacy of your bathroom. Don't expect long-lasting miracles from this wrap, though, because it draws toxins out of your fat cells and helps them shrink for only a day. (But hey, sometimes that's what you desperately need!) The magnesium in the Epsom salts also brings down any inflammation you may have going on. Do this the night before your event so you can more easily slip yourself into that dress, skirt, or skinny jeans.

WHAT YOU DO

I like to measure my waist, hips, thighs, and even my upper arms before I do this wrap so I can see the difference when I'm done. Combine the ingredients in either your bathroom sink or a large bowl filled with warm water. Soak the bandages in the solution and wrap your naked body in them, starting at your ankles and going up your legs, then torso, arms, chest, and shoulders. Make sure it's not uncomfortably tight. Cover it with a layer of plastic wrap so you don't drip everywhere, or just stand over a towel in the bathroom. You can also throw a robe over the whole thing. Try to keep moving for 30 minutes while still wearing the wrap. Don't work out vigorously, but don't sit down and lounge either. After a half hour, remove the wrapping, standing in the bathtub because the salt will flake off. Take your measurements again. Amazed? I hope so! Take a warm, steamy shower afterward.

Body Bliss Treatment #2:
The Dandelion Bloat-Buster Tea

Dandelion root tea has proven itself to me as a stellar bloat buster. It gets rid of excess water and is a natural diuretic (so get ready to visit the ladies room a few times!). Go for an organic brand, and either you can buy the herbs at a health food store or you can find just the tea bags at many grocery stores. Drink it at least once daily leading up to the big night. It also works great for that special time of the month when bloating seems to linger. Bye-bye, protruding belly—you are not our friend! (On a side note, if I need a tiny bit of sweetness, I'll add a little organic stevia or some honey in the tea. And as silly as it might sound, I have a self-stirring mug that I found online, and it works great for this.

Body Bliss Treatment #3:
The No-Bloat Pre-Party Food Guide

Bloating is a topic close to my heart as well as my tummy. There's nothing more hellacious than trying on a gown the night before an event and looking like a sausage! Good news: It's never too late to lose the bloat, so rather than get discouraged, why not take the bull by the horns? In the five days to one week leading up to an event, you can accomplish so much in your mission to look stunning in that dress. Try on your outfit, and then follow this eating guide for the week. You'll be so Blissful when it fits better and you look like you've been slimming down for much longer!

Low-fat Greek yogurt: This stuff fills you up, thanks to its protein. The probiotics help keep your tummy flat and slim. Other dairy products can produce gas and bloating, but Greek yogurt actually helps reduce it. This week, your only dairy food should be Greek yogurt.

Strawberries: You may remember that in Face Bliss you learned that these beautiful berries can whiten your teeth, but they're also high in H_2O, so they help keep you hydrated and glowing. That's not all: They rev up your metabolism and make you feel fuller.

Asparagus: It might make your pee smell funky, but eat plenty of it this week because some research shows it has probiotic properties (helps with bloating) and can reduce gas and help your system flush out toxins. It's high in fiber, which also keeps things moving, thus keeping your waistline slim.

Watery fruits and veggies: Think of produce like watermelon, celery, cucumber, and grapes as your best friends this week. Load up on them to reduce puffiness all over your hot body!

Water: Drink a lot of it...and don't undo all the Bliss it provides by eating a lot of salt or drinking alcohol or caffeine since all of those are very dehydrating. Also, avoid drinking water during your meal—instead, have a glass 20 minutes before and after your meal so as to not inhibit your digestion.

Garlic: Put it on everything this week because it's a natural diuretic (remember you want to flush your system this week), and it helps burn fat.

Cinnamon: Sprinkle it on your Greek yogurt or put it in your smoothie for another fat-burning boost.

Lean meat once a day: Eat your extra lean meat like turkey, chicken, or white fish in the middle of the day instead of at night. Go for a veggie-only dinner this week. And don't prepare your protein with a lot of oil. Limit that to just 1 teaspoon per day. Hey, it's only a week!

Green tea: I love this stuff. It's so packed with healthy antioxidants, and it just makes me feel good. Have 2 cups per day this week, and don't sweeten it except for with a sprinkle of cinnamon if you'd like. If you don't love the taste right away, you'll learn to love it soon.

Parsley: Chew on a sprig of parsley, or chop it up and throw it your salad; either way, this fresh, fragrant herb is a natural diuretic, so get plenty of it this week.

When it's party time, you can even further enhance the results from all the work you've done by picking up a body-shaper garment to go under your party dress. These come in all types, shapes, and price ranges nowadays. I love ones that have tummy-flattening panels—sometimes they're just what I need for an extra boost of confidence.

Have Your Sweet Bliss and Eat It Too

There's a war on sugar, in case you haven't heard. The battle lines are drawn, and you're either on Team Sugar or Team Sugar Is the Devil. I choose to be Switzerland in this particular war. I don't believe it's realistic to tell anyone (least of all, myself) to stop eating sugar permanently. Where would you draw the line anyway? By cutting out all high-fructose corn syrup products? OK, but what about refined sugar products? Then, do you get into all the other names for sugar: sucralose, barley malt, cane sugar, caramel, carob syrup, dextrose, maltodextrin? Do you study the label of every single food you purchase? What about those foods that turn into sugar in your body like white rice or white bread? I don't know—it's just a lot to think about, and all these potential rules just add to the never-ending inner food dialogue we already have in our heads. I want to quiet that conversation so you can just eat food and enjoy life. But I also know you can't ever truly experience Body Bliss if you're weighing yourself down with barrels of sugar that we know causes energy crashes and weight gain. It's a sugar conundrum. Alas, I have a reasonable solution.

Here's your body Bliss guideline when it comes to sugar: Listen to your taste buds. What are they telling you when you bite into that muffin, sip that soda, or munch on that protein bar? If it tastes crazy sweet, it's either loaded with sugar or laden with chemicals that aren't doing your body any favors, so put it down. Do your best to eat most of your foods in their natural state, not processed, and by doing so, you'll automatically eat less sugar overall without even really thinking about it. When you start tuning your taste buds, you'll soon find that the sweet foods you once craved are now overwhelming and unappealing. With every sip I bet you'll be thinking, "One hour 'til I crash—who needs that?" When you do need to sweeten up a smoothie or add something to your tea, consider reaching for a little raw honey or organic stevia, both of which I consider to be Bliss Foods.

Body Bliss Sugar Solution:
Organic Stevia

I blame my Scottish heritage for my over-the-top sweet tooth. But to avoid the extra calories of refined sugar, I'm a fan of stevia (the organic variety), and I think you will be too. I use it as a substitute for sugar in my tea, and I mix a little into my yogurt or smoothie—there are many different uses for it. From a health perspective, it doesn't do that sugar-high-and-crash routine because it doesn't cause a spike in your blood sugar the way refined sugar does. But remember to trust your taste buds—you don't need a lot of this stuff. Just a little bit goes a long, sweet way.

Body Bliss Sugar Solution:
In the Raw Honey

Raw honey is almost like reaching right into a bee hive and pulling out the honeycomb. It's often found in a jar instead of a squeeze bottle, and it's usually cloudy or even white because it hasn't been pasteurized or processed in any way so all its nutrients are intact. But the same rule applies: Don't overdo the honey. A tiny bit will get the job done.

. . .

I have encountered so many women who let an obsession with their bodies leach out every ounce of Bliss from their very bones. I know all the reasons why we do it (boy, do I!)—from the social pressures to be thin to the fears about weight-related health problems—but none of those reasons make it OK for us to walk around unhappy because of the shape, size, and feel of our bodies. So, from now on, every time you make the decision to grab something healthy or burn a few extra calories, take a moment to be proud of yourself. And every time you give in to temptation to skip the gym or down a cookie, don't sink into the guilt quicksand. Just put that little slipup into an imaginary helium balloon and let it go. You are an awesome, powerful, bright, and beautiful woman all wrapped up in a body that is unique to you. Celebrate that Blissful bod of yours!

Chapter 8

Beauty Bliss Plan

OK, dolls, without any further ado, now it's time to put into action all the ingredients I've given you for Bliss. The goals of this seven-day routine are to prepare yourself, from head to toe, for the 30-day Bliss Plan. In other words, you'll clean out your pores so that the skin treatments in the Bliss Plan work even better, you'll start laying the groundwork for feeling inner Bliss, you'll probably lose a few pounds as you start attaining Body Bliss, and so on. Trust me—this week will put you on the path to Bliss, and you'll start noticing results almost immediately by following my daily routine. Prepare to be amazed because reaching your goals will be way easier than you could imagine. (And don't make me remind you about the Bliss Pact you signed!)

Beauty Bliss Deal-Breakers

A few things can make or break this week for you. These tidbits are things you need to do every day in conjunction with the daily plan. It all works together in harmony, ladies.

Daily Must-Haves

Nix *"Debbie Downer" Foods* and add more *Bliss Foods* (on page 80) to your everyday diet.

- Drink 8 cups of water to keep your body fully hydrated, thus improving the appearance of your skin, helping decrease hunger pangs, and helping you feel better in general.

- Replace your morning coffee (which can stain your teeth) with a *Rise 'n' Shine Mint Lime*.

- Reduce salty foods to get rid of puffiness and bloat.

- Snack on plenty of *Crunchy Munchies* (on page 51) to help whiten your teeth.

- Reduce or completely cut out alcohol.
    - I know this can be a bummer, but the idea is to clean out your system, and if you're guzzling wine or margaritas, that's harder to accomplish.

- Make sure you're taking the proper dosage of vitamins and supplements (on page 27).

- Don't use any heat tools or styling products on your hair. (If you just choked a little when you read that, I understand! But this sacrifice will be worth it, I promise.)

- Stimulate healthy hair growth by giving yourself a daily two-minute scalp massage. Or maybe there's someone who can do this for you!

- Start your *Bliss List* (on pages 17-18) and add something to it each day, even if it's just one line.

- Got all that? Good, because Day 1 starts right now!

Day 1

Today's Date: _____

My Current Bliss Factor: _____

Drink a *Rise 'n' Shine Minty Lime*. (Recipe on page 88.)

What is your number-one Bliss goal for this week? (Remember: Push yourself to get out of your comfort zone, but also be realistic.) _____
_____

What will your 22 minutes of *Bliss-ercise* be today? (Examples on page 90.) _____

Today's skin treatment: *Ooh-La-La Lavender Pore Cleanser* (Recipe on page 33.)

Take seven minutes at some point today to turn off all the sounds of your life, including the TV, music, phone, computer.... Take a break from family and friends too. Just be still and quiet. Tune in to your inner voice, and think about what you really want, what will truly make you Blissful. Get as specific as you can—what will your Bliss look like, and how will it make you feel?

Today's body treatment: *The Mystical, Magical Epsom Salt Bath*. (Recipe on page 93.)

Record one or two things that happened today that made you feel Blissful. It could be a fleeting moment of time or hours on end—try to pinpoint and describe it.

Today I felt Bliss when: _____
_____
_____

Remember: You should be adding to your Bliss List (on pages 17-18) each day.

Day 2

Today's Date: _____

Upon waking, enjoy your *Rise 'n' Shine Minty Lime* drink (recipe on page 88) instead of coffee.

Are you holding a grudge or carrying negative thoughts?_____

_____

_____

Now, say it and then immediately say "Over it!" You've just let it go for good. If the negativity tries to make a comeback at some point, remember that you've already gotten over it, and move on from it.

What will your 22 minutes of Bliss-ercise be today? (Examples on page 90.) _____

Today's hair treatment: *The Once-a-Month Hair Bliss Boost.* (On page 61.)

(*Note:* Since you're not using heat tools this week, when you're done with this hair treatment, try separating your hair into two parts, twirl it around your fingers so it's twisted, and then clip up the two sides and let them dry. Yes, you'll look like Princess Leia for a little while, but it will help keep the frizz away and give you more manageable hair throughout your heat hiatus.)

Find the prettiest shade of red lipstick you can and write on your bathroom mirror as you say this out loud: "You are gorgeous!" Say this out loud every time you go into the bathroom.

Today's skin treatment: *Ooh-La-La Lavender Pore Cleanser.* (Recipe on page 33.)

Today I felt Bliss when: _____

_____

_____

Day 3

Today's Date: _____

Upon waking, enjoy your *Rise 'n' Shine Minty Lime* drink (recipe on page 88) instead of coffee.

I am grateful for: _____

_____

What will your 22 minutes of *Bliss-ercise* be today? (Examples on page 90.) _____

Drink the *Dandelion Bloat-Buster Tea*. (Recipe on page 95.)

Today's body treatment: *The Buttermilk Soak*. (Recipe on page 39.)

Today's skin treatment: *Ooh-La-La Lavender Pore Cleanser*. (Recipe on page 33.)

My Bliss declined when: _____

_____

_____

The next time that happens, I'll handle it by: _____

_____

_____

Today I felt Bliss when: _____

_____

_____

Day 4

Today's Date: _____

Upon waking, enjoy your *Rise 'n' Shine Minty Lime* drink (recipe on page 88) instead of coffee.

I will give bliss away to someone else today in the following ways: ____

_____

_____

What will your 22 minutes of *Bliss-ercise* be today? (Examples on page 90.) _____

Do: *The Incredible Shrinking Woman Wrap.* (Recipe on page 94.)

Today's skin treatment: *Ooh-La-La Lavender Pore Cleanser.* (Recipe on page 33.)

Today I felt Bliss when: _____

_____

_____

Reminder: Have you been adding to your *Bliss List* each day?

Day 5

Today's Date: _____

Upon waking, enjoy your *Rise 'n' Shine Minty Lime* drink (recipe on page 88) instead of coffee.

How are you sabotaging your Bliss? What are the excuses you tell yourself for why you can't be happy, healthy, and beautiful? Or, how have you been procrastinating and what are you putting off?

_____

_____

Now, write down how you can overcome this excuse. For example, if your excuse is that you're too busy to focus on yourself, you would overcome this by resolving to make yourself a priority and finding the time. _____

_____

_____

Today's skin treatment: *Ooh-La-La Lavender Pore Cleanser.* (Recipe on page 33.)

What will your 22 minutes of *Bliss-ercise* be today? (Examples on page 90.) _____

Today's nail treatment: *Strong As Nails Weekly Soak.* (Recipe on page 72.)

Today I felt Bliss when: _____

_____

_____

Day 6

Today's Date: _____

Upon waking, enjoy your *Rise 'n' Shine Minty Lime* drink (recipe on page 88) instead of coffee.

What will your 22 minutes of *Bliss-ercise* be today? (Examples on page 90.) _____

Today's skin treatment: *Ooh-La-La Lavender Pore Cleanser.* (Recipe on page 33.)

How will you give Bliss away to a stranger today? Get creative! _____

_____

_____

Drink *The Dandelion Bloat-Buster Tea.* (Recipe on page 95.)

Were you your own worst Bliss frenemy at any point today? How?

_____

_____

Today I felt Bliss when: _____

_____

_____

Day 7

Today's Date: _____

Upon waking, enjoy your *Rise 'n' Shine Minty Lime* drink (recipe on page 88) instead of coffee.

What will your 22 minutes of *Bliss-ercise* be today? (Examples on page 90.) _____

Today's skin treatment: *Ooh-La-La Lavender Pore Cleanser.* (Recipe on page 33.)

Remember, don't be hard on you: Even if you didn't follow this Bliss Beauty Plan to a tee, be proud of what you were able to accomplish. Get excited for the next phase, and stay committed to finding your Bliss. Right now, give yourself a pat on the back and tell yourself, "You're amazing!"

Today's body treatment: *The Mystical, Magical Epsom Salt Bath.*

Today I felt Bliss when: _____

_____

_____

Write down the positive changes you've made this week. Did you lose a few pounds? Is your skin looking healthier? Do you feel more grateful? Is your hair shinier? Did your nails grow? Did you achieve your number-one Bliss goal for the week? Take notice of all changes, big or small.

_____

_____

_____

· · ·

After you complete the Beauty Bliss Plan, it's time to start adding Bliss to your home, relationships, energy, and all areas of your lifestyle so you can then immediately embark on the Living Bliss Plan, which starts on page 111. There's no time to waste; your next weeklong party should start tomorrow, so keep that momentum going.

Part 3

Living Bliss

Now that you're feeling great and looking beautiful, let's shift our focus just a tad and tackle areas outside of your skin and hair. In this part of the book, you're going to learn how to truly set yourself up for Bliss—the kind that seeps through your pores no matter where you are. Look around the room you're in right now. Do you like what you see? Do you feel Blissful being in this space? The truth is it shouldn't matter if you're sitting in a motel room, a university library, a subway car, or your very own living room. Wherever you go, you have the ability to change your environment in ways that will bring you Bliss.

What about your energy? I'm referring not only to the amount of energy you have throughout the day but also to the energy you're giving off to others. Are you mostly feeling anxious, nervous, or feels, too, because the type of energy you feel inside is the same energy others get from you. Remember when we talked about inner Bliss and edgy? Or perhaps you feel lazy, lethargic, or idle—like you're just sort of along for the ride? Then that's what everyone around you how the more Bliss you give away, the more you naturally receive? I want you to experience and accept Bliss from all angles of your life, but first you have to learn how. Changing your energy may feel like a monumental task, but it's not.

By now you know I am all about simple solutions, and this is no exception. Bliss can be contagious, especially among couples. When Jerry is having a great week, I share in his victories and success, not just as his partner and friend, but I feel the excitement in my own bones. And when I'm feeling especially Blissful, he also reaps the rewards. In Living Bliss, I designed a chapter with information you can use for or with your partner. Of course, I'm not here to dish out marriage advice. My goal is to show you fun, creative Bliss tips to help you connect with your lover or partner. But it mostly comes down to how you can laugh together and enjoy each other. Sure, I'll help you cure the acne your man has on his back, but I'm pretty confident you'll both be cracking up the whole time. Laughter is the outward expression of Bliss, and it's always better when you're sharing it with someone.

And moms, you get your very own chapter. I know firsthand how much your life changes when kids enter the picture. I'm here to encourage and motivate you to be the best, most loving mother ever, but you may be surprised by my method because it starts with putting—and keeping—yourself at the top of your priority list. That might sound impossible: I mean, how can you work, get your kids to soccer, buy groceries, clean the house, manage the finances, and find time for yourself? It is possible, I promise!

For those of you who have pets, you know how much they add to your overall Bliss. No one in the world is happier to see you when you come home than your pet! But sometimes the ins and outs of pet ownership can get a little tiresome, so I'll give you all kinds of great ideas, tricks, and simple tips to enhance your relationship with your pets so that your own Bliss Factor can keep growing.

Once you've read these chapters and started to truly understand how to maximize your Bliss, then you'll start the one-week Living Bliss Plan, which will get you primed for the 30-day Bliss Plan! Think it sounds simple? That's the point—it is! Let's continue, shall we?

Chapter 9

Environment Bliss

Your environment is vital to your Bliss. By "environment," I mean your home (every room in it, even closets), your car or other forms of transportation, your office, anywhere else you spend time, and I'm even including clothes and accessories in this category.

Consider this question: What are you consuming? I don't mean just the food you're eating, but what are you consuming with your other senses? What are you touching, looking at, listening to, and even smelling? All of that is part of your environment. Just like the food you eat has an effect on your body, everything you're taking in from your environment has an effect on your mind and, thus, your Bliss. But you have control over your environment. And it doesn't have to be expensive to change it.

Think of how you feel when you walk into a messy living room, with clothes strewn about, take-out containers left behind, bland colors on the walls, and mismatched furnishings. Doesn't exactly inspire Bliss, right? Now imagine walking into a bright, neat room with delightful décor. You wouldn't mind spending time in that room, right? You could stretch out on that couch with a good book and enjoy a couple hours of peace and quiet. I'm letting out a deep sigh just thinking about it. Not every room needs to inspire relaxation; perhaps, for example, you have one room that is your favorite place for getting creative. The point is that your outer environments are a reflection of your inner Bliss. If you're unhappy, very often your home often reflects that state of mind.

Along those same lines, your home can and should be a predictor of what you're planning for next. Remember, I want you to constantly listen to your inner voice about what will bring you Bliss and take steps to go after that goal. This includes setting up your various environments to be conducive to achieving your Bliss. In my case, when Jerry and I decided to have a child, we moved out of an ultra-modern condo that wasn't ideal for raising kids and into a house that felt more like a cozy cottage. Of course, that didn't help us conceive, but it did help us wrap our heads around where we were headed and our shared goals for our family. I know moving into a new home isn't always an option, but you can transform your current home or environment to match what you have decided to go after. It could be as simple as painting some walls, moving some furniture, or creating more space by getting rid of clutter. It's amazing how even minor changes can make a major impact.

No matter where you go, whether it's a business trip that lands you in a dingy hotel room, a train ride into the big city, or just walking into your own kitchen, you have the power to change the space around you and make it work for you. With something as simple as a soothing scent, a favorite shirt, or music that makes you smile, you can change your experience and, in turn, your Bliss. OK, let's start working on your environment Bliss right now!

Feathering Your Nest

Decorating your home or office so that it's Blissful doesn't have to include hiring a celebrity interior designer and spending your retirement on some funky new couch. Challenge yourself to stretch your dollar and find unique furnishings that you can individualize so they fit into your environment. Here are my top five favorite methods for creating a happy, homey space that reflects your personality.

Top Five Interior Bliss Tips

#1: Hit Up Flea Markets

You can find all kinds of unique home accessories at flea markets and yard sales. Take a cell phone photo of the area of your house that needs spicing up so you can look at it while you're shopping. This way, you're more likely to pick something that will fit in well! And remember—you can always add a coat of paint or stain to spruce up a great (and cheap) find.

#2: Find Inspiration Online

There are a gazillion blogs and websites chock-full of unique and crafty ideas for turning trash into treasure. I recently saw a super-cute piece of art made completely out of free paint samples you can get at a home-improvement store. I mean, come on! The possibilities are endless.

#3: Less Is Best

Accessorizing is fun, but try not to go too crazy with the knickknacks when you're feathering your nest, or else it could start to look and feel like clutter. Aim for your home to feel open, clean, and Blissful by not overdoing your décor.

#4: Add Pop with Patterns

Don't be afraid to mix stripes and solids, animal prints, and plaids. Combining various patterns keeps your home interesting and stimulating.

#5: Decorate with All Five Senses

Personalizing your home isn't just about the colors and furnishings you see. Utilize your sense of smell with scented candles or oils, your sense of touch with textures like silk and faux furs, your sense of hearing by having soft music or sounds of waves playing on a loop in certain rooms, and even your taste buds by keeping healthy Bliss Foods out in pretty dishes or bowls.

Hints for a Happy Home

From the moment you pull into the driveway or walk through your front door, you should feel welcomed and comforted, not stressed out by chaos. If you walk into a space that doesn't give you a sense of Bliss, your emotional reaction to whatever is thrown your way will be negatively impacted. But if you enter without tripping over toys and feel a sense of peace as you look around, you're more likely to be calm, cool, and collected when your dryer and dishwasher simultaneously go kaput, a circuit breaker blows, or your A/C goes out in the middle of a heat wave. Ugh!

Color palettes play a gigantic role in how you feel inside a space. Experts have shown that the color of a room can do everything from make you feel hungry to put you right to sleep. So, why not use this information to your advantage and create the type of Bliss you're looking for in every part of your home? I call it stacking the deck in favor of your Bliss. Also, simple organization techniques can give any space a neat, tidy feel that helps you feel peaceful and relaxed.

Living Room Bliss

This space should be where you and your family can kick off your shoes, play games, veg out on the couch, and, well, live! You can achieve that type of living room Bliss by employing warm, earthy colors such as brown, beige, rust, or orange tones. Some research even shows that this palette can encourage people to open up, chat, and converse with one another. General clutter, an overabundance of toys, too much furniture, or even too many things hanging on the walls will create a feeling of chaos. Your living room should reflect you and your family at your very best. Listen, I'm not telling you how to decorate—just giving you the research, and the rest is up to you.

Bedroom Bliss

This should feel like your sanctuary—the place you can go to fully decompress and leave the craziness of the day behind. I enjoy sleep so much, don't you? When I'm sleeping well, I perform at my best in every area of my life. The best colors to help you achieve a peaceful night's sleep are cool colors such as lavender, blue, and shades of gray. Clutter in the bedroom can cause anxiety (which will affect sleep!), so keep your dressers, nightstands, drawers and even the space under your

Where Your Environment and Beauty Converge

Your bedroom is where you get your beauty sleep, and they call it that for a good reason, mostly because when you don't get a good night's sleep, it's pretty obvious. Crusty, bloodshot, puffy eyes with black bags under them, a look of exhaustion, or even confusion—yep, they're all telltale signs that Mr. Sandman did not bring you Blissful dreams last night. Gosh, don't you just love it when someone says, "Hey? Are you feeling OK? You look...tired." They might as well say, "You look terrible!"

Well, here's a simple tip on how to make the most out of your beauty sleep. If you use a smooth, satin pillowcase, it can help minimize the appearance of the fine lines on your face. And it can help reduce the bed-head effect by not ratting up your hair every time you turn over. Who knew?

bed as neat and organized as possible. You have a laundry hamper, so use that instead of the floor for dirty clothes! Also, cover your basic bedroom needs such as good lighting, books, relaxing music, an alarm clock that doesn't shock you into your first moment of wakefulness in the morning, and a couple luxuries (such as a super-soft throw blanket, scented candle, or a beautiful plant) around the room. Envision a room in a five-star hotel, and try to capture that feeling in your very own bedroom. Blissful dreams!

Kitchen Bliss

Your kitchen can be about so much more than where you cook and eat. It should be a place where there's happiness and a feeling that everyone can be "nourished" here. Color accents in the kitchen can range from canisters on your counter to towels hanging on your oven, or you can paint cabinets and walls. Red is a bold, invigorating color but—beware—it can make you hungry! Yellow is a cheery, sunny color that can put you in a great mood and open up the space.

Undo Cooking Boo-Boos

Greasy Pan: Fix it with ¼ cup baking soda and a couple capfuls of hydrogen peroxide. Make a paste, rub it on the greasy areas, and watch the mess disappear.

Stuck-on Food: Fill the pot or pan with water, add a fabric softener sheet, and then soak overnight to loosen the food particles. Or try denture-cleaning tablets in water for the same effect.

Burned Dinner: Rid your kitchen of burned-food smell by adding slices of orange or lemon to a simmer pot of gently boiling water. Pretty soon, the whole house will smell like a citrus grove.

Home Office Bliss

This is where you likely need to focus your mind and accomplish tasks. If you're easily distracted, go for neutral colors in this space. But if you're seeking inspiration, go green. Decorating with green accents might help you get creative and concentrate for a long stint at the computer.

Your work area in the home can be a magnet for a multitude of documents, sticky notes, mail, and an endless amount of paper-related chaos. Many people have the tendency to just create stacks of papers thinking they'll get to them eventually, and before they know it, the stacks take over the room (or the house)! Work on creating a functional system that works for you, not against you. Organize this space using inboxes, bulletin boards, filing cabinets, baskets, or magnetic boards so you can designate a "home" for each and every type of paper that is coming in and going out of the room. Not only will this keep the room looking nice, it will also reduce your risk of overlooking an important task or bill. I like to use bright, colorful files because they inspire me and even make me look forward to organizing. To further reduce the potential for clutter, find ways to go paperless. Whether it's your credit card statement, electric bill, or car loan, many of these companies now offer to email you the information. If you're the kind of person who needs to hold the piece of paper in your hand, consider investing in a paper shredder so you can quickly and safely dispose of unneeded paperwork. Just file away what you want to keep, and shred what you don't. You'll be far more productive in your lovely work space!

Bathroom Bliss

For many women, especially moms, the bathroom is truly the only place you can go to be alone with your thoughts. Maybe your bathtub is your place of Bliss, where you can go to escape and unwind. Like every other room in your house, you'll get the most enjoyment out of this space if you keep it clear. This includes your countertops, so it might mean finding new ways to hide the stuff that typically ends up there. Do you really use all five bottles of perfume you have sitting out?

Wash Away Water Spots

Hard-water stains all over your faucet can take away from your bathroom Bliss! Here's a simple hint: Cut a lemon in half, and rub the lemon right on those spots and rinse. See spot disappear! When it comes to stains or soap scum on a shower door, try cleaning with a dryer sheet. Simply dampen the sheet, start at the top of the door, and wipe your way down. This works best if you do it often, before the scum can really build up. Another option for shower doors is to douse them in rubbing alcohol and wipe them right off. (Make sure the space is well-ventilated! You don't need to be getting high off the fumes.)

Can you just throw out the tube of mascara that has goop coming out of the sides? Is there a "home" you can find for the aromatherapy gift you got six months ago but haven't opened? Scale everything down to what you really love and use the most. Use baskets, plastic bins, and organizing trays to keep things together in your cabinets and drawers. Just go back to that five-star hotel room or to your favorite spa in your mind and use it as inspiration here, too.

In setting up your most Blissful bathroom space, keep in mind that cool and clean colors such as white, turquoise, blue, and green tones all promote relaxation. Calgon, take me away!

Kids' Room Bliss

When it comes to children's rooms, you want to pick energizing colors that will stimulate their growing brains. Just think about an elementary-school class room—it's a collage of primary colors. But you also want it to go well with the rest of your home, which probably doesn't include every color of the rainbow. Consider opting for neutral wall colors, but use bright, primary, stimulating colors in the bedding, art, furniture, accessories, and other décor.

It's a Toy (Storage) Story

Toys spread all over the floor and stuffed haphazardly into shelves don't instill Bliss in you as a mom, and it doesn't send a great message about order to your kids either. Here are a couple simple and creative ending for the same old messy toy story. First, hang an over-the-door shoe rack on the door and use the shoe pockets to stow away dolls, stuffed animals, and so on. Another super-fun idea is to install magnetic strips on the wall and use them to keep metal toys or cars. Velcro strips on the wall also work great for plush toys. Or you can use colorful baskets, buckets, or bins to store groups of toys. I love stackable bins because they maximize your space. Label these storage bins or baskets so you know exactly where to find what you need, and it makes cleanup easier on the kiddos. As for bath toys, a hanging fruit basket on the shower rod is a great place to keep rubber duckies so they can dry out (otherwise they get moldy—yuck!) and stay out of sight.

Closet Bliss

Remember on *Friends* when Monica wouldn't let anyone open her "Monica closet"? Even someone as Type A and organized as she was had one area that was overflowing with junk! Sound familiar? We all want to keep our home looking put-together and clean, but inevitably we end up with at least one place where all the leftover, uncategorized stuff that you just can't seem to throw away or find the right spot for gathers together in a sort of unholy congregation of clutter. For some, it's just a "junk drawer," but for many of us it's an entire closet with that anxiety-provoking designation. (Or the whole garage!) I think closets can be a major source of stress in our lives—if we let them. They can get so out of control that you dread even the thought of having to get dressed in the morning because you know you'll break into a sweat searching for what you want. Well, the first step is to get out of denial. Walk-in closets are called *walk-ins* because you're actually supposed to be able to go inside! If you can barely wedge one foot in, it's time to fill up a few trash bags and donate what you don't need. And by "need" I mean that if you haven't touched it in a year, chances are good you can live without it. But let's move past that.

I want to really empower you with some tips from an expert, so I am sharing a professional organizer's top tops. Stacy Thomes, founder of the Los Angeles–based company Strive to Organize, is a business owner, wife, and mom of two young kids, so she understands what it's like to be crazy busy. Her passion is helping women simplify their lives, and here's what she recommends:

- ◉ **The first step is to believe that you can be organized.** Maybe you think the ability to organize is a gene that you just weren't born with, but the truth is, anyone can do it. You just have to find a method that works for you!

- ◉ **Less is always more.** Most people don't even come close to wearing every item in their closet regularly, so keep only the items that make you feel great about yourself like the clothes that fit properly and give you confidence. Give the rest away. Also, if you lose weight, don't keep those oversized clothes! Treat yourself to something new that accentuates your fabulous new body. It will make you feel great and inspire you to hang on to your new figure.

Cleaning Supply Solution

When you open up the cabinet under your kitchen or bathroom sink, do oodles of cleaning-supply bottles tumble out? What if you could move them to another space entirely? Simply hang an over-the-door shoe organizer on the inside of your laundry room door and give each bottle its own slot. Suddenly you can actually see everything (so you don't purchase your third bottle of glass cleaner just because you couldn't find the other two), and the real estate under your sink is wide open. Don't have a laundry room door? No problem—just cut the organizer in half and hang it on the inside of your under-sink cabinet doors. How 'bout them apples?

- **The one-for-one rule: When you buy something new, remove one (or more!) item from your closet.** A good way to do this is to keep only a certain number of hangers in the closet, so if you're out of hangers, you know it's time to give something away.

- **If there's a pair of shoes you haven't worn once in six months to one year, give them away.** Be honest with yourself: Are they uncomfortable, too high, out of style, or too trashed to wear? You know, deep down, if you aren't going to wear them again. As long as they're not totally ruined, I guarantee someone else will appreciate having them.

- **Do a closet edit every three to six months.** Give yourself a realistic timeframe to get the job done, make the date in your calendar, and then just get in there and do it. Create three piles: keep, donate, and toss. If you do this consistently, each session won't take very long.

- **Keep your hangers uniform.** Mismatched, random hangers take up a lot of precious space in your closet, prevent you from seeing your clothes clearly, and just look disorganized. They're not expensive, so resist the urge to hang onto every hanger that comes your way.

- **Keep like items together in your closet, and then organize them by color.** For instance, keep your long-sleeved shirts together grouped by color so you can easily find your favorite green shirt. The same rule applies to dresses, skirts, pants, short-sleeved shirts, and so on. Your closet will also be aesthetically pleasing when you organize it this way, and you'll spend much less time looking for what you want.

- **If you have the space, move last season's clothes to the back of your closet or another closet so that this season's items are front and center.** There's no reason to comb through wool sweaters when you're trying to find your favorite linen summer dress. In fact, during the spring and summer months, consider keeping thick sweaters in zippered fabric boxes (preferably labeled) and moving them into a coat closet, garage, or anywhere else that's out of the way.

- **Try using pretty boxes or baskets to store loose items in your closet.** Having attractive methods of storage will help motivate you to stay organized because you won't mind spending time in that space.

I think everyone has experienced an unorganized, chaotic closet from time to time. Don't let yourself get overwhelmed with the prospect of cleaning it out. Just take deep breaths and conquer the clutter one step at a time. These tips will get you on the road to a full closet recovery. You can also find out more about Strive to Organize at www.strivetoorganize.com.

How to Cut the Clutter

Whether your clutter is out in the open, shoved in a coat closet, crammed in a junk drawer, or maybe even cordoned off in an entire room (caution tape, anyone?), clutter definitely won't enhance your Bliss. I don't know about you, but sometimes I think I can actually hear my junk drawer calling out, "Clean me! We're all suffocating in here!"

Decluttering doesn't have to be a full weekend affair. Try taking small steps. Set a goal for each day: Maybe clean out all the jeans in your closet one day, and then focus on a particular stack of paperwork or mail the next day. I realize this can be a very emotional process. We're a nation of consumers, and it's very easy for us to get attached to our stuff. But keep in mind as you clear out items like clothing you no longer need that there are many underprivileged people who could benefit greatly from them. Try to remove yourself from the excuses preventing you from just letting go. Trust me; you'll feel so much better when your space is clear, clean, and functional.

You'll also find plenty of specific tips for clearing out the clutter in the Living Bliss Plan. With each tiny piece of clutter that you throw away or find the perfect place for, do a little happy dance and congratulate yourself. Even the little victories count!

Your Home Away from Home Environment

Remember, wherever you go, your environment goes with you. You can spice up, calm down, and personalize pretty much any space you're in. It can be as simple as carrying a relaxing scent around in your purse.

The first step is to realize that you deserve to be Blissful wherever you go. Once you do that, you'll find that it's actually easier than you might imagine. Think about the time you spend anywhere other than at your home such as a hotel, a family member's house, or your office. Empower yourself to set up your space so that it makes you smile with these tips:

- **Mini speakers** are a great way to play music that makes you feel more at home anywhere you go. There are many varieties, with a price range starting at $10 for travel speakers up to super pricey for high-end ones. If you need to wind down, try soothing nature sounds such as waves or rain. Or if you need to pump it up early in the morning, go for some Top 40 favorites.

- **Travel candles** often come in little tin containers with lids, and you can choose from a myriad of scents that can instantly energize, relax, or invigorate you.

- **Bedding** is more portable than you think. Sometimes just bringing your own pillowcases can create a whole new comfort to a hotel bed. Or take it a step further by bringing your own sheets or a throw blanket.

- **Fave foods** or drinks are always smart to carry with you. Bring your favorite tea packets when you're on the go, or prepare snacks in plastic bags so you're always prepared for the munchies and not as tempted by the snacks in the mini bar or vending machine.

- **Flowers or plants** help to boost your Bliss in any space. Whether it's a couple of cut tulips in a water bottle in a guest room or a lucky bamboo plant on your desk, there are tons of options for plants to brighten up a space.

- ⊙ **Memories of home** will always put a smile on your face. Stash a small framed photo in your suitcase of your spouse, siblings, kids, pets, or whomever it is that puts a smile on your face so it goes wherever you go. Or, keep a few photos in your purse to look at any time.

- ⊙ **Beauty routines** aren't just for when you're at home. Bring your favorite products or treatments in travel-size containers. Beauty Bliss can happen no matter where you are!

Be on the Bliss-Dressed List

Did you know that you can greatly increase your chances of success in an interview, on a date, or in a meeting just by wearing the right color? It's true. In fact, there are certain shades you can wear to boost your Bliss in many different ways. Ask yourself, what is your power color? What is the one color that makes you stand up straighter, feel more confident, and go out there and own it, no matter what "it" is? I think everyone has a color like that.

Studies show that wearing red can make you pay more attention to details and focus more on accuracy. Red is definitely a powerful color—it can ignite passion and energy. I personally love wearing red; it makes me feel more sure of myself and puts a smile on my face.

When you wear the color blue, you might feel more creative and imaginative. So, if you're looking for inspiration and motivation, reach for the blue-toned clothes in your closet.

But when the pressure is on and the stress is high, you might need to wrap yourself in a color that brings you down a notch and makes you take a deep breath. We often associate green with nature, so it gives off a fresh, renewing feel.

Whatever color you choose to wear, I think it's best to dress primarily for yourself. In other words, we all like getting a compliment about how we look, but wearing something that makes you feel good should be your primary goal. Think about what colors give you Bliss first, and then consider how you might want to affect others. Whether you're going on a date, hosting a party, or attending a meeting, what message are you trying to send?

Your Blissful Car Atmosphere

Depending on where you live, you might spend just as much time in your car as you do anywhere else! I live about an hour from Hollywood, and I'm constantly commuting, so my car is a pretty big part of my life (if I had a nickel for every time I've been in bumper-to-bumper traffic on the Hollywood Freeway...). So, I know how important it is to create a comfortable environment in your car so that the crazy traffic doesn't turn you into a raving lunatic!

Whenever I appear on talk shows, I bring a whole slew of stuff with me ranging from wardrobe and shoes to homemade concoctions of beauty remedies, wacky new products, bowls, and blenders—you name it, and I've probably stuffed it in my car. One helpful producer offered to help me unload when I arrived at a studio last year, and when he saw how packed to the gills my car was from the front seat to the trunk, he turned and said, "Kym, your secret is safe with me. You're homeless and living out of your car!" I knew he was kidding, but sometimes it really does look like I'm living out of that thing! Alas, most of the time I try my best to follow my own advice in the Car Bliss category. Here are my top five tips.

Top Five Car Bliss Fixes

#1: Music to Soothe the Soul

Especially if you have to drive long distances or sit in stop-and-go traffic, I think having options for music is really crucial. It's smart (and safe) to preset your favorite radio stations, CDs, or MP3 player lists so you don't have to search around for them while you drive. Make sure you choose a variety—sometimes you might need some classical to keep

Don't Pay a Cent to Fix That Dent!

If you have a dent in your car from a little oopsie in the grocery store parking lot, here's a trick you just have to try before you take it to the body shop. Grab a toilet plunger and place it over the dent, push it in to create suction, and then pull it off. In most cases, the dent will pop right out. Of course, it depends on the size and severity of the dent, but this is definitely worth a shot.

the road rage at bay, other times you might be in the mood for a book on CD, and occasionally you gotta pump it up with some Katy Perry! Furthermore, if you have kids, radio programs tailored for them can really grate on your nerves. So, I suggest getting your kid an MP3 player and letting them listen to their own, kid-friendly tunes with headphones in the backseat while you enjoy something a little less, well, annoying while you play chauffeur.

#2: Keepin' It Neat and Tidy

It's never fun to open the driver-side door and see the remains of yesterday's protein shake in the cup holder, toys strewn across the floor, or fast-food wrappers stuck to the seats. You can keep your car looking like the day you drove it home from the dealership with these simple tricks. First, buy a plastic cereal dispenser or just reuse a plastic bag and turn it into a trash receptacle you can keep in the back seat. Make sure everyone knows that's where they're supposed to stuff their junk! Then, every time you return home, empty the trash. It takes just a few seconds, as opposed to climbing in and searching around for everyone's messes. Also, keep a stash of baby wipes in your center console and use them to clean up the dashboard, the insides of your doors, armrests, and anywhere else there could be dust, spills, or unidentifiable sticky disasters. For leather interiors, rather than pay a pricey car wash to detail your interior, simply mix up one part gentle laundry detergent (only the kind you use on delicates) with six parts water and give your leather a nice cleaning. Just rub it on with a sponge, and then wipe off. Cleaned and conditioned leather will make you smile. One more thing: I'm sure you already have hand sanitizer in your car. (If not, you should—it's great to use after you pump gas.) Here's a whole new use for it! The high alcohol content helps dissolve and remove stains, spills, and the occasional ink spot on upholstery.

#3: Bug-Free Bliss

It's the worst when a big, fat bug smashes right into your windshield and no matter how many times you wash it off with the windshield wipers, it just smears around more and more. Ick! That'll surely steal your Blissful mood, especially if it affects your ability to see the road. But here's a simple anti-bug tactic: Keep some fabric-softener sheets stowed away in the car (and I really do mean stowed away—put them in the glove box instead of leaving them loose). Take one out when you get to your destination and get it a little damp with some water. Then, quickly rub it in circles on the bug gunk, and it'll come right off. You can also use this technique when you actually wash your car. Bye-bye, buggie!

#4: Protect Yourself (and Your Bliss)—Be Prepared

Part of feeling great while you're driving yourself and your family down the highway is knowing that you're prepared for anything—from a minor boo-boo to a tire blowout. Get a plastic medicine kit and fill it with items such as cleaning wipes, hand sanitizer, lip gloss (you never know!), bandages, antibiotic cream, pain reliever, antihistamines, and, my personal favorite, sunscreen (because our hands are exposed to sun while gripping the steering wheel). It's also super smart to have jumper cables and a cell phone charger on hand. Depending on your climate, you may need to have blankets, candles, and lighters stowed away in the car just in case of a snowstorm! Of course, also make sure you're taking your car in for routine oil changes or checkups so it's as safe as possible.

#5: Cheerful Scents

In the car, it's best to pick scents that invigorate and energize—after all, you don't want to be falling asleep behind the wheel. I like to dab some essential oil under the floor mats and seats and even rub a little into the steering wheel! The best scents are citrus, particularly orange, because they boost your mood and make you feel naturally energized—jasmine because it makes you feel more awake and alert by increasing your brain's beta waves and cinnamon because it may increase dopamine in the brain, perking you up and even possibly improving reaction time.

If you're traveling in a plane, train, subway, or bus, you can still make the ride more comfortable. Dab a favorite scent on your wrists or behind your ears, bring a neck pillow, escape into music through your headphones, or do whatever it takes to create an environment and experience that increases your Bliss.

. . .

Have you ever driven somewhere that you go often, arrived, and then realized that you don't even remember driving there? No kidding, I have driven home from taping a television segment at one of the studios in Hollywood, pulled into the driveway, and wondered how I even got there! I think that's a perfect example of how so many of us are just going through the motions, day in and day out, like zombies. So engrossed in our own thoughts (and cell phones), we hardly notice what's going on around us. We choose to simply ignore the messy living room, the cluttered closet, or the strange scent emanating from the floor mats in our car. Well, now is the time to use all of your senses and decide whether all of your life's environments are adding to your Bliss or subtly robbing you of it. Once you know, you can start to make the changes I've suggested in this chapter. You'll be amazed what joy even the smallest adjustments can bring you.

Chapter 10

Energy Bliss

What do I mean by Energy Bliss? I'm referring to all the types of energy that affect your life on a daily basis that can either fuel your Bliss or zap it completely. Here's an example: I believe that it takes more energy to be rude than it does to be kind.

I say all the time that you get more bees (and people) with honey than vinegar. But that's easier said than done when you're having a particularly low-horsepower day or you're at your wit's end. That's where my plan comes into play. There are simple things you can do to feel more alert and invigorated, which will likely make you give off a nicer, less prickly energy to others around you. (Store clerks, customer service reps, and bank tellers everywhere will thank you.) But it's not just about others—it's about liking your energy for your own sake because it's no fun being with yourself when your energy is negative.

Anxiety can be an insidious form of energy. Perhaps you're the worry wart in your family or group of friends. You love to be in control of every tiny detail in your life (and sometimes the lives of those around you!), even the things you can't actually control. Or maybe you're just susceptible to the occasional attack of nerves (who isn't?). I'll give you some simple solutions to help you let go in moments of sheer fret, worry, and uneasiness.

There's one component of my plan that applies across the board: sleep. Every single one of us needs a good night's sleep on a regular basis. It's not just me telling you that; there's research to prove it. That's why sleep is an essential ingredient in the recipe for Blissful energy. Oh my, how I adore sleep. Isn't it the best? A good, solid, uninterrupted night's sleep is like pure gold. Sometimes I have my best ideas when I'm dreaming...if only I could remember them. Kidding! But I'm excited to share some fabulous secrets sure to improve your sleep so you can have more energy to run your life every day. So, come on, it's time for an energy Bliss makeover.

Get a Lift!

Tired, shmired! Let's get you lifted with some all-natural shots in the arm for pure energy Bliss without guzzling gallons of pricey energy drinks that can have some negative side effects like giving you a major case of the jitters or disrupting your sleep. When I've had a particularly busy week, sometimes even the fun dinners or parties we've been planning to attend on a Saturday night seem like a chore. I'll try to back out of them so I can just crawl under the covers and flip on the tube. But then I think about how excited I'd been when we'd made the plans, and I pull myself up by my bootstraps, do a quick face mask, and pull myself together. You know what else I do to find renewed energy? Glad you asked! Here are some tricks that work well for me.

Energy Bliss Treatment #1:
Channel Your Inner "Glee"

Did you know that something really cool happens in your body when you sing? Your stress hormones even out, and you can actually create a sort of emotional high out of thin air! You don't have to have pipes like Mariah Carrey or Carrie Underwood in order to sing out loud and proud. Whether it's in the shower, in your car, or in your living room with a hairbrush microphone, perform your best *American Idol* audition. (Hey, maybe all that practice will make you the star of the karaoke bar!) The same is true for playing music—I find that blasting some tunes and dancing changes my whole mood.

Energy Bliss Treatment #2:
Use Pressure (the Good Kind)

You may have heard there are certain points on your body that can calm you down when you apply a little gentle pressure. I found out years ago that this works to relieve headaches, but it can also give you a nice little pep in your step. Simply squeeze the fleshy area between your index finger and thumb. It works best for me when I squeeze super hard. Hold on for a minute or two. Now go out and be the Energizer bunny!

Energy Bliss Treatment #3:
Take a Hike

This can be a literal hike, or you can just get up and walk around. I have friends who turned into long-distance runners simply because they needed a way to increase their energy. I know it seems a little counterintuitive—get up and move when you're completely exhausted? But if you're expending energy, your body will work harder to create more of it. In fact, just a ten-minute walk can boost your energy in a way that lasts up to two hours (and the benefits increase even more if your walk is outdoors).

Energy Bliss Treatment #4:
Get Nutty

Nuts are like little energy powerhouses. When you're feeling droopy, drag yourself into the kitchen and snack on a handful of nuts. Almonds and peanuts are especially high in magnesium and folic acid, which play a role in your cells' production of energy. Pretty cool, right? I recommend going for the raw, unsalted variety (remember, salt is the enemy when it comes to bloating!). Needless to say, ignore this tip if you have any nut allergies.

DIY Blissful Energy Bars

I know they are quick and easy, but many of the energy and protein bars on the market are pretty high in sugar, sodium, and fat—not to mention how expensive they are! Why not just make your own energy bars? You'll save money and calories. Play around with the ingredients until you love them, but the *Kiwi Lime Bliss Bars* and *Banana Bliss Bars* are high in fiber, plant protein, healthy fats, B vitamins, antioxidants, magnesium, and more—all of which help your body create natural energy among other health benefits.

Kiwi Lime Bliss Bars

WHAT YOU NEED

1 cup dates, pitted, whole

1/2 cup raw cashews

1/2 cup raw almonds

2 tablespoons unsweetened shredded coconut

3 teaspoons fresh lime juice (can also use grated lime zest)

2 kiwis, peeled

WHAT YOU DO

Preheat the oven to 350 degrees. Combine all ingredients in the food processor, but add kiwi last so it doesn't get goopy. (Don't forget to remove the pits from the dates!) Pulse slowly so the mixture remains chunky. Remove from the food processor, and spread over a thin baking sheet that's been sprayed with nonstick spray. Pop it in the oven, and bake them for 25 minutes. Then, flip the whole mixture over (you may have to cut them into slices), and bake them for another 15 minutes so the bottom isn't mushy. Slice into bar-size pieces. Yum!

Banana Bliss Bars

WHAT YOU NEED

1 cup dates, pitted, whole

1 cup raw almonds

2 bananas

WHAT YOU DO

Preheat the oven to 350 degrees. Combine all ingredients in the food processor, but add banana last. Pulse slowly so the mixture remains chunky. Remove from the food processor, and spread over a thin baking sheet that's been sprayed with nonstick spray. Bake for 25 minutes. Then, flip the whole mixture over (you may have to cut them into slices), and bake them for another 15 minutes so the bottom isn't mushy. Slice into bar size pieces. Delish.

Curb the Nerves

In case you missed my story about what happened before the first time I appeared on *Ellen*, I tend to have a nervous stomach. Over the years, I've gotten much better at taming the anxiety so it doesn't completely block my Bliss. The truth is, I still occasionally get fraught with nervousness and have to work hard to talk myself out of having a throw-up session. But for the most part, I've found a way to channel the anxious energy and use that spike in adrenaline. I can actually feed off of it to accomplish more, get more creative, and push myself further by transforming the anxious energy into positive adrenaline to my advantage. Here are some of my go-to solutions.

Energy Bliss Treatment #5:
Quick Energy Conversion

If your energy is registering super anxious, try a simple conversion. Sometimes getting rid of that nervousness can be as simple as wearing yourself out physically. Going to the gym is great and all, but it's not always at your fingertips. Why not stand up and do two sets of 50 jumping jacks? Anything physical that gets your blood pumping for a few minutes will help calm your mind and your nerves.

Energy Bliss Treatment #6:
Sip Your Nerves Away

There are nerve-settling benefits to drinking antioxidant-rich green tea or chamomile tea. Green tea often has caffeine, so depending on your state of mind, you may want to pick a caffeine-free variety instead. Chamomile tea is herbal and naturally caffeine-free. Neither of these drinks will put you to sleep, but they will soothe your racing mind. (Bonus: When you finish the cup of tea, you can cool the tea bags in the fridge for a little while and then lay them on your eyes to relieve puffiness!)

Energy Bliss Treatment #7:
Comic Relief

If you've ever seen me on *Ellen*, you can probably tell that I truly believe laughter can cure almost anything. Life has so many funny moments along with the inevitable times that if you don't laugh, you'll cry. (While my first choice is always to laugh, sometimes the crying is automatic and inevitable.) If you're feeling anxious, find something, anything, to giggle about. One thing that always works for me is watching a funny movie.

Whether your idea of a good comedy typically stars Adam Sandler or Bill Murray, pick out a classic, sure-to-crack-you-up flick, and watch at least a few scenes. Let yourself laugh out loud because all those endorphins the laughter creates helps to normalize your stress hormones and bring your anxiety level way down. Don't have time to watch the whole thing? Then hop on YouTube and scroll through the millions of hilarious videos until you find one that makes you LOL. There is even a website that lists the week's funniest tweets from around the globe. Laugh a little, and you'll likely feel less stressed and ready to tackle the issue at hand or at least keep it in perspective— sometimes that's all we can do.

Strike a (Yoga) Pose

Some of the best bodies I've ever seen are yoga bodies. It's been around for centuries, and there's good reason. Not only is yoga excellent exercise, but the fluid movement and concentration it takes to hold some of those poses also help to alleviate feelings of angst or anxiety. You don't have to sign up for an expensive yoga class to enjoy the benefits, though. Here are some of my favorite poses that I do in the comfort of my own home!

Downward Dog: This is a great way to get some blood flowing to your brain, stretch, and elongate your back and hamstrings. Create an upside-down V with your body by placing your hands flat on the floor and your feet as flat as you can get them, depending on how tight your hamstrings are. You may need to bend your knees a bit at first. Keep your head between your arms and your butt straight up in the air. Take several deep breaths in this position.

Bridge: This gets the blood flowing in your thighs, which is invigorating. Lie down on your back, and then bend your legs and slide your feet in toward your butt. Then lift your hips high off the ground, squeezing your butt and keeping your arms by your side. Stay there for three breaths, and then release. Repeat several times, breathing deeply the whole time.

Child's Pose: With your arms fully extended in front of you and your forehead on the floor, bring your legs underneath your torso. Keep stretching your arms and back while pulling your hips down to your feet. Deeply inhale and exhale several times. I get so relaxed in this position I could practically fall asleep!

Sleeping Beauty

I think of a good night's sleep as sort of like shaking an Etch-a-Sketch. (Remember those?) Say your day has been just rotten to the core. You've been a big bundle of nerves, you've hit nothing but red lights (both on the road and metaphorically speaking), your skin is broken out, and your sister is blowing up your phone asking for man advice. When your head hits the pillow, you get to shake the Etch-a-Sketch clean, wipe away all the negativity, and start fresh to draw a whole new picture in the morning. (I'm not saying all the circumstances will change, but your mind-set and overall energy certainly can.) But you don't get to hit the reset button if a restful night feels like a hopeless proposition. Here are my favorite simple methods that are sure to help you get the rest that your mind and body need. (There's a reason it's called "beauty sleep!")

Energy Bliss Treatment #8:
Adopt a Pre-sleep Ritual

- Your body craves routine, so if you can manage to go to bed around the same time every night, you'll likely go to sleep faster. Likewise, if you do the same things every night before bed, your brain will know sleep is coming soon to a theater near you and start winding down. Here are some ideas for pre-sleep rituals. Spray a tiny bit of lavender water on your pillow. The soothing scent of lavender has been used for ages to help people get to sleep.

- Turn on a white noise machine or a fan in the bedroom. This will drown out any other noises that might disrupt your sleep without you even realizing it.

- Do a few gentle stretches. Studies show that women who stretch regularly report improved sleep.

- Shut off the cell phone, laptop, or tablet because they only add to anxiety. Whether you're trying to knock things off your to-do list until the moment you conk out or just emailing friends doesn't matter; you have to power down and so do your electronics.

· · ·

I love to be around people who have strong, positive energy. There is something almost palpable when I'm in the same room as someone with that indescribable "oomph." It fills me up and ignites my own energy. Indeed, your energy level is susceptible to so many variables, such as the kids having a meltdown, how your thyroid is functioning, or the traffic jam that has you running 20 minutes late for an important meeting. But the goal here is to put yourself in the best possible position for anything and everything that life hands you. The only thing you can control is you, so complaining about external factors isn't nearly as productive as doing all you can to help yourself. Figure out which lifestyle changes will put you in the best position for your own Blissful energy to emerge. You will soon see the impact it has not only on you but on everyone around you.

Chapter 11

Man Bliss

This chapter is called "Man Bliss," but you don't need a significant other in your life who's a man to reap the rewards here. Perhaps your other half isn't male or there's no guy in your life right now or you choose to be single. Cool! The goal is to find fun ways to connect with someone important to you, or you can use these treatments on yourself!

I live for romance in my life. Yes, I'm a hopeless romantic; it's just how I'm wired. But I actually prefer to call myself a hopeful romantic. I mean, seriously; I married a soap star, and he's been my husband for more than 25 years. For us, it's the everyday little things that keep our romance alive and love in full bloom. The other day, when I was completely swamped with work and stressed to the max, I mentioned offhandedly that a smoothie sounded so good but I just didn't have the time to make one or grab one at a shop. Sure enough, 15 minutes later, I turned around, and Jerry was holding my favorite raspberry smoothie.

Before the word "smoothie" had fully left my mouth, he'd jumped in the car and gone to get me one. I'm telling you—that was the best-tasting smoothie in the world because of his thoughtfulness. By the way, it was less than three bucks, proving that expressions of true love don't have to come with a high price tag.

Here's another perfect example that it really is the simple things we do for one another that has kept our relationship strong and alive. Every once in a while, for no reason at all, he leaves me little poems on my pillow or my dresser, like this one I have saved for a long time and reread constantly:

You tease me with your eyes

and thrill me with your kiss.

You impress me with your mind

and remind me love is Bliss.

OK, I'll snap back to reality—I know every day isn't a scene out of a chick flick or soap opera in my life or anyone else's. In the real world, poems don't appear on your pillow or flowers at your door every day, and relationships aren't perfect. They will always have their ups and downs, but as the poem says—love is most definitely Bliss.

But this isn't a chapter on love; it's a chapter about our guys, who, for many of us, are the objects of our love. Yes, we adore, admire, and enjoy them, but sometimes they are in need of some general improvements, right? To be clear, by "improvements," I'm not referring to changing his personality flaws, faults, and defects. If those are the types of issues you're dealing with, I recommend that you mosey on over to the Dr. Phil section. But if you've been contemplating how to help him tackle that yucky "backne" breakout, improve the appearance of his positively stinky, cracked, dead skin-laden feet, or you're seeking new ideas for getting Blissfully frisky with him, then this chapter has your name all over it. Ultimately, I want to introduce you to some super-fun techniques from which you'll both give and receive some Bliss or that you can use on yourself.

Right off the bat, let's put it out there that unless you are dealing with a metrosexual, your guy probably isn't going to instantly embrace the concepts I mention here. However, with a little coddling and the right timing, he will warm up to the idea if you make it appealing. Suffice it to say that you shouldn't bum-rush him with a pair of nose hair clippers and a box of hair dye. You know that isn't going to end well. However, even if he says he doesn't care about his appearance, he will be offended if you tell him that the blackheads on his nose are huge or that his breath smells like old pizza. There are subtler ways to get him on board with making some improvements. And, girls, once he sees the positive effects, your handsome devil will be asking you for a mud mask. No kidding!

This chapter is not just about your boyfriend or husband—it can apply to all the men in your life. You can even work this magic on your son! I hope this doesn't embarrass Hunter, my teenage son (sorry, honey!), but I think it will give you some insight into how the tricks in this chapter can help the man (or men) in your life. And you'll see that they secretly want to look good, but they're just afraid to ask how. Hunter and his school friends were all hanging out at our house. I noticed they had been getting breakouts on their foreheads from wearing football helmets and getting all sweaty after the long hours of practice. They're all around 14 or 15 years old, and they're starting to "hang out" with girls on a regular basis, so their appearance is becoming a higher priority than it's ever been before. When they casually mentioned to me in their macho way that they wanted to fix their skin, I went into Bliss Mom mode and practically sprinted into the kitchen. I whipped up a sports mud mask from the fridge for the entire JV team. There they all sat, the 155-pound, 6-feet-2-inch sweaty, dirty, smelly teenage boys, anxiously waiting in line for me to slather my homemade concoctions onto their faces on the family room couch. It worked like a charm, and they were firing up the computers to Skype with their female friends in mere minutes. (You'll find the recipe in this chapter.)

The bottom line is that men want to look great just like women do. In fact, in the United States, men spend $84 million a year on high-end skin care products geared toward dudes. And men now account for one-third of all spa-goers. Male-centric terms have been coined from *manscaping* to *BROtox*, and if I had to guess, I'd say this trend is only going to grow. But, again, I'm here to save you money and show you healthy, natural alternatives to some of the pricier, chemical-based beauty (or, in this case, handsome...or even "man-some") routines.

The first step is to try to think like a male. Clearly, they aren't going to be partial to some kind of treatment with a girly name, so the *Ooh-La-La Lavender Pore Cleanser* won't be on the top of his list of favorite things to do on a Sunday afternoon. That's why you'll find that the names of the treatments in this chapter are geared toward guys. Words like *athletic*, *sports*, or even *bomb* are manlier, so they'll be more receptive to it. Because my husband is a soap-opera actor, he's used to having someone put makeup on him or style his hair, so he doesn't cringe if I want to put a little mask on his nose to get rid of some blackheads. We used to joke that he'd show up far more made up and put together for parent-teacher conferences because he went to the school right from the set, whereas I'd go right from an exercise class. Lovely!

Breakouts Affecting Makeouts?

Intimacy can be a challenge if his face is peppered with pimples. Of course, you'll love him regardless, but you might find yourself staring at the zits on his forehead, unable to tear your eyes away, much less bring yourself to snuggle up with him. It's like when someone's kid is having a massive meltdown in line at the grocery store—you don't enjoy watching, but you just can't seem to stop gawking. Rather than dabbing some of your concealer on it while he snoozes on the couch, hoping he doesn't notice, try this method. Focusing on his eyes instead of the offending pimple, tell him he has just the tiniest (even if it's the size of Mt. Vesuvius) blemish and you'd like to help him dry it out and clear it right up in no time with a *Sports Mud Mask*. And promise not to tell anyone, especially his fantasy football league.

Sports Mud Mask

WHAT YOU NEED

2 tablespoons honey

1 kiwi

1 teaspoon cinnamon

This combo of honey, kiwi, and cinnamon packs a powerful punch to collections of bacteria harbored on your man's face and in his pores. Honey acts as a natural antimicrobial while simultaneously locking in moisture so he doesn't get those unsightly dry patches. Kiwi (remember—this is my favorite "super fruit") is loaded with vitamin C, which will help exfoliate dead skin, lighten up problem areas, and give his skin a sexy glow. Cinnamon can plump out the skin and bring the blood to the surface, thus minimizing fine lines. Some studies even show that cinnamon has antibacterial properties.

WHAT YOU DO

Mash up the kiwi with a fork, and combine with the honey and cinnamon. Have him wash his face using a gentle facial cleanser or coconut water first so his pores are primed and ready. Then, use your fingers or a small paint brush to evenly spread the mask on his forehead, nose, cheeks, and chin. The mask might get runny on his warm skin, so it's best to have him lie on his back so it doesn't drip into his eyes. Leave it on for 20 minutes, and then have him rinse off with warm water and a wash cloth, using gentle, circular motions. His pores will be smaller, and the skin will be cleaner and tighter right away!

Are His Feet Interfering?

Have you ever been watching TV and glanced over at his bare feet propped up on the ottoman and decided he needed a feet-ervention? Unkempt feet can really kill the mood...any mood! Whether they're just rough around the edges or need a total overhaul, these tricks will get his tootsies back on the path to handsome right away.

Are Those Toenails...or Claws?

If his toenails have you wondering whether he's moonlighting as a werewolf, it's time to take some action. You may need to use some gentle manipulation, such as, "Honey, I have an idea. How about you give me 15 minutes so I can give you an athlete's pedicure, and I promise it will include a foot massage. And it involves beer." And maybe that massage will lead to a little romance too!

Man Bliss Treatment #1:
Athlete's Beer Pedicure

WHAT YOU NEED

Toenail clippers

Nail file

Shallow basin filled with warm water (or just use the bathtub)

1 bottle (or can) of beer

A few drops of shower gel

1 teaspoon coconut oil

Cuticle stick

Unscented lotion

2 drops eucalyptus oil

Towel

This isn't exclusively for the athletic type; it works great on everyone. But it sounds so macho, doesn't it? The beer isn't just for fun, either. It actually contains B vitamins, which are great for the skin, and they soften calluses. The hops in the beer also moisturize, while the alcohol acts as a natural antiseptic. Once again, I recommend coconut oil because it's majorly moisturizing and has antimicrobial qualities, so it'll help protect his feet and toenails from bacteria and fungus. I like the eucalyptus oil because it smells masculine.

WHAT YOU DO

Fill a shallow basin with warm water and a full bottle or can of beer. Alternatively, fill the bathtub with just enough water and beer to fully immerse his feet. Before he puts his feet in the water/beer combo, clip his toenails to a good length, and file the edges so they're not sharp. Don't cut them too short, or he'll be more prone to ingrown toenails. Then, have him soak his feet for five minutes. Lightly towel them dry, but make sure the toes remain damp. Now that the cuticles are soft, rub them with a little bit of coconut oil, and gently push them back. Optional: Rub his feet for a few minutes with the lotion, mixed with the eucalyptus oil. Rinse them off completely and towel dry.

Hitting a Rough Patch

The only thing worse than getting cut by his razor-sharp toenails under the covers is when his rough heels actually cause snags in your sheets! If your guy has such dry heels that they're actually splitting and causing fissures, here's a helpful routine you can help him adopt.

Man Bliss Treatment #2:
The Handsome Heels Technique

WHAT YOU NEED

Pumice stone

Heel file (found at most drug stores)

Coconut oil

2 hand towels soaked in hot water

Depending on how bad his heels have gotten, this may take several sessions, but you're sure to see results right away. Yet again, coconut oil comes to the rescue. Once you've removed the dead skin with the file and pumice stone, the oil will penetrate deep into the dry skin and help prevent cracks in the future.

WHAT YOU DO

The object of this game is to remove as much dead skin from his heels as possible, and then replace it with some serious moisture. While his feet are dry, use the heel file to remove the dry, flaky skin. Do this over paper towels because otherwise there will be skin everywhere! (If he does this on his own, encourage him not to do it while watching TV in the living room, unless he plans to vacuum up the mess.) Avoid areas with deep fissures, because this may irritate them further. Then run warm bath water over the feet and scrub them gently with a pumice stone. Leave the stone in the shower and encourage him to use it every day on his heels while showering. Then, pat dry his feet and slather on plenty of coconut oil, making sure to get it in any heel cracks he may have.

Wrap his feet in the warm, wet hand towels (make sure they're not too hot), and let it all soak in for 15 minutes. Remove the wet towels and wipe off the excess coconut oil with a dry towel. Have him put on socks right away so his heels can continue to soak in moisture. If he's willing, put coconut oil on his heels at night and then put socks on. This will help avoid the dry, cracked heels in the future!

Corns No More

If he (or you) suffers with ugly corns or calluses, try mixing a few drops of licorice root extract with 1/2 teaspoon sesame oil. Rub it into the hardened skin on your foot or toes. Cover with a sock and let it soak in overnight. The phytoestrogens in the licorice help to soften up that hard, tough skin, and the sesame oil adds plenty of moisture.

Odiferous Feet Fights

If his stinky feet are so potent you can smell them a mile away, don't overreact and give him a smelly foot complex. And remember, your favorite pair of high heels probably don't leave your own feet smelling as fresh as a daisy either! It's always a smart move to sprinkle a little baby powder in the worst-offending shoes so it can soak up the odors and add a fresh scent.

Man Bliss Treatment #3:
Top-Shelf Odor Killer

WHAT YOU NEED

3 cups vodka

2 cups water

1/2 cup olive oil

2 teaspoons crushed mint leaves

4 drops eucalyptus oil

When smelly feet strike, simply pull out the vodka! No, not to drink—to kill the stink! You might want to buy the cheaper kind so as not to waste the good stuff. The high alcohol content of the vodka is excellent at killing odor-causing bacteria, and the mint and eucalyptus leave his feet smelling fresh and clean.

WHAT YOU DO

Stir the ingredients together in a large bowl. Pour half of it into a plastic grocery bag (make sure it doesn't have any holes first!), and put his foot in the bag. Tie it tightly around his lower calf so it stays secure. Repeat the same procedure for his other foot. Have him sit on the side of the bathtub to do this, in case of any spillage. Have him soak his feet for 15 minutes, and then thoroughly rinse them off. The odor is gone!

Low-Maintenance Manscaping

Not all guys are willing to engage in a little bit of manscaping here and there. If yours is a just-the-basics soap and water kind of man, then you may have to go the extra mile to help him embrace the concept of prettying himself up occasionally. The key is to have these items in the house, at the ready, for when a little extra grooming opportunity presents itself. Here are a few common issues men (and, yes, women) sometimes encounter and my simple, inexpensive solutions.

Man Bliss Treatment #4:
Cool Your Pits Odor Fixes

Sweaty armpits can cause your man to smell pretty ripe, especially if the sweat is from stress. You know how sometimes the cure is worse than the ailment? Some of these may seem that way at first, but they're all worth it! Depending on the severity and how much time he has, you can choose which option is best for him. The salt in the tomato juice will balance his skin's pH and help eliminate the odor for a longer period of time.

Option 1

WHAT YOU NEED

2 paper towels

1/4 cup apple cider vinegar

4 cups tomato juice

WHAT YOU DO

Wipe his underarms with a paper towel soaked in apple cider vinegar. No, he won't smell like a jar of pickles all day, but the acidic pH of the vinegar will kill the bacteria in his pits. Then, run a warm bath and pour in the tomato juice. (He might feel like he's been sprayed with a skunk.) Let him soak in it for 15 to 20 minutes.

Option 2

WHAT YOU NEED

Orange peel from 1 large orange

WHAT YOU DO

Rub the outside of the orange peels on his armpits several times. The peel's dimples help exfoliate the skin. The citrus scent makes him smell fresh and fragrant.

Man Bliss Treatment #5:
Bad Breath Banishment

Especially if your man's diet consists of a lot of meat (and not enough flossing), bad breath can happen, and it can definitely have an effect on intimacy between the two of you. In the following fixes, you'll find parsley, which is high in chlorophyll, a natural deodorizer for bad breath. There's also lemon, which will kill bacteria growing in the mouth, and salt, which can help remove food particles in between teeth. Finally, vodka comes to the rescue again! But neither of you wants to drink this alcoholic mouthwash. It's just meant to kill germs lurking between teeth and around the mouth.

Option 1

WHAT YOU NEED

Several sprigs of fresh parsley

Salad or veggie side dish

WHAT YOU DO

Chop up the parsley and add it to his salad or side dish with dinner. Alternatively, have him chew on a sprig of parsley for a quick breath freshener.

Option 2

1 lemon

Table salt

WHAT YOU DO

Slice the lemon into a wedge. Sprinkle salt all over the lemon wedge. Have him put the wedge in his mouth, holding it between his front teeth. Have him suck on it for a few seconds. This works particularly well after a garlicky meal or a meal with lots of onions.

Option 3

WHAT YOU NEED

1 cup vodka

9 tablespoons cinnamon

WHAT YOU DO

Mix the vodka and cinnamon together, seal in an airtight container, and refrigerate for two weeks. Strain the liquid through a coffee filter. Mix the fluid with a little water, and have him rinse out his mouth with it for 15 to 30 seconds. It will burn a little because of the alcohol content, but it leaves his breath smelling cinnamon fresh!

Stimulate His Hair Growth

Thinning hair or hair loss can be a big hit to the male ego. (By the way, millions of women also suffer with thinning hair or hair loss.) If he's experiencing either of these, the solution might be hiding in quite an unexpected place: a bottle of prenatal vitamins! They're chock-full of essential vitamins and minerals that can help hair and nails grow at an astounding rate, but I'm not suggesting that he start raiding your

When Backne Attacks

Acne on the back, or *backne* (whomever coined that term is so clever!), is very common. It can occur because of irritation from detergent in his clothes or dry-cleaning solution, an accumulation of sweat, or stress. If this is an ongoing issue with him, definitely try switching to a dye- and fragrance-free detergent and a mild, moisturizing soap in the shower.

It's also possible it's just in his genes, but regardless of the cause, you can help! Here are several ways to decrease your man's odds of back breakouts and control them when they flare up.

Man Bliss Treatment #6:
The Backne Bomb

WHAT YOU NEED

1 tablespoon apple cider vinegar

4 tablespoons water

Several cotton balls

If he's currently broken out on his back, this is a great way to make the zits disappear in a hurry. Don't pop the pimples (even though I know some girls love doing that!) because that can make them worse or even make them bleed. No blood on the shirt, please! Apple cider vinegar is the active ingredient in this backne bomb, and that's because

medicine cabinet to pop your pills. Instead, get either capsules or liquid prenatal vitamins, and put the bottle in the shower. Have him massage one dose into his hair after shampooing and leave it in for a couple minutes before rinsing out. If he's consistent, you might just start seeing shinier, healthier hair and more of it in as little time as two weeks.

it kills bacteria, absorbs excess oil, and causes the pH level of the skin in that area to become very acidic. The bacteria that cause the zits in the first place can't tolerate this acidic environment.

WHAT YOU DO

Mix the water and apple cider vinegar together, and then dip a cotton ball in the solution and hold it on the pimple. Check to see whether it's causing any irritation. If so, don't hold it on there for more than a couple of seconds. If not, hold it on there a few seconds longer. Wait five minutes before rinsing the area so that it can fully soak in. Use a cotton ball dipped in water to rinse it off. Repeat this procedure in the morning and at night.

Man Bliss Treatment #7:
Tactical Backne Prevention System

WHAT YOU NEED

3 tablespoons brown sugar

1/2 cup rolled oats

How's that for a hard-core name? Sounds like a way to prevent nuclear war, right? Even if he's not currently broken out on his back, this prevention system is a great way to reduce the number and severity of his breakouts. The sugar and oats act as natural exfoliants, removing dead skin cells and thoroughly cleansing his skin. Plus, they aren't as irritating as many "manly" shower gels you find at the supermarket, with all their fragrances and additives.

WHAT YOU DO

Combine the oats and brown sugar in a bowl. Have him get in the shower and get his back wet with warm water. (You can get in the shower with him for this treatment or stand outside and reach in through the curtain or door.) Rub the mixture all over his back, lightly scrubbing in circles. If he's not in the shower, it's best to have him lying down for this. You might have to add water to the mixture if the dampness of his skin isn't enough to turn this into a paste. If you're concerned about oatmeal and sugar going down your shower drain, you can do this in the bathroom, with a towel on the floor. It's messy—but just have fun with it! After he rinses it all off, moisturize his back with an unscented lotion (for fewer irritants) or use a little bit of coconut oil as a moisturizer. Coconut oil has some antimicrobial properties, so it can further help his skin resist bacteria.

When Backne Moves Down South

If your man suffers with breakouts on his behind, he might have what I affectionately refer to as *buttne*. It happens to everyone, but men are more prone to it because they're more likely to sweat in the butt area. Plus, if he works out or plays sports without immediately jumping into the shower, bacteria can thrive and cause pimples. It's nothing for him (or you!) to be embarrassed about, but it's definitely a problem worth treating.

You might be the first to notice when it's his behind that's broken out, so if you spot a blemish, try handling it with a tad more finesse than pointing at it and squealing, "Ew! Disgusting! You have a giant zit on your butt!" Trust me; he's no more enthused about it than you are. Once you've alerted him to the issue by nonchalantly mentioning it the next time he's getting dressed, offer him these solutions (and your assistance, if he's willing to let you help), and no one gets humiliated.

Man Bliss Treatment #8:
The Buttne Be-Gone Strategy

WHAT YOU NEED

Half a cucumber, sliced

Half an avocado

1 teaspoon coconut oil

2 tablespoons aloe vera gel

If he's currently under attack from a barrage of butt pimples, it's best to start with the *Tactical Backne Prevention System* so the area can get exfoliated. Then, hold ice cubes on any swollen, red pimples for at least 30 seconds each. This will help reduce the swelling. Follow it up with this deep cleansing mask for the behind. Yes, this whole thing probably sounds absurd—both of you should laugh your way through it and just get silly!

The cucumber is a great natural astringent, the coconut oil and the aloe vera both have antibacterial/antimicrobial properties, and the avocado provides nourishment and moisture to the skin so it doesn't dry out and the oil glands don't go into overdrive, leading to breakouts. Yes, he's probably going to feel like you're putting a pureed salad on his bum, which you sort of are! But it's cooling and relaxing, so have him lay down on a towel and get a magazine or good book to read while you slather this on and let it soak in.

WHAT YOU DO

Puree the sliced cucumber, avocado, and coconut oil in a food processor or blender until it is smooth (you may need to add 2 tablespoons of water to get it to a good consistency). Mix in the aloe vera gel. Then gently apply it to his butt cheeks, using an upward motion. (You should both be cracking up during this process!) Allow it to soak in for 15 minutes. Then, thoroughly remove with a wet washcloth or paper towel. His cheeks will be glowing!

Man Bliss Treatment #9:
The Fundamental Butt Facial

WHAT YOU NEED

Gentle facial cleanser (like one you'd use on your face)

1 cup coffee grounds

5 aspirin

A few drops of water

Gentle moisturizer

Cool Down That Razor Burn

Like most of the treatments in this chapter, this one definitely applies to men and women alike. No matter where you might get razor burn on your body, an aspirin paste can soothe the pain and relieve the red bumps. Just like it helps relieve an inflamed pimple, aspirin is an analgesic and anti-inflammatory, so it relieves both the pain and irritation.

This is a daily zit deterrent he can use to keep from breaking out on his, well, his gluteus maximus, to begin with. Many high-end spas are now offering similar treatments to their patrons, but here's one you can do right at home. (Save your money for the date night you'll want with your butt-zit-free man!) Consider doing a couples butt facial! You can do this once a week to keep the skin on his (and your) butt soft, moisturized, and pimple-free.

WHAT YOU DO

Crush up the aspirin and mix with a little water until it's a paste. Set aside. Cleanse the area with a gentle facial cleanser you'd use on your face. Then, get the coffee grounds damp and rub them in circles to exfoliate his buttocks. Don't scrub too hard as to irritate the skin. Rinse off or wipe off the coffee grounds with warm water or a warm wash cloth and then apply the aspirin paste, particularly to areas prone to breakouts. Allow it to dry, which takes about five minutes. Then wipe off with warm wash cloth and apply a gentle moisturizer you'd use on your face or a few dabs of coconut oil. Now his behind is squeaky clean and much less likely to break out.

Blissfully Frisky Foods

If you're looking for ways to boost romance, you might think of the typical aphrodisiacs like oysters or champagne and strawberries. But there are other, far more unexpected, foods that could have a positive effect on both his and your desire to, eh hem, you know, get frisky with each other!

Celery: Ha, I know—celery probably isn't the first food you think of when you're trying to get your man in the mood! Just imagine greeting him at the door wearing a pair of heels and an apron, with a celery stalk in your hand. Not super-romantic. But when men eat celery, it can boost their arousal, causing them to release a certain hormone that acts as a pheromone. That pheromone can then cause a woman to be even more attracted to him. Crazy, right? Everyone wins!

- ⊙ **Recipe Idea**: Make a fresh, crunchy salad to start off a romantic meal. Include chunks of celery, chopped roma tomatoes, fresh shredded basil, crumbles of herbed goat cheese, and a little olive oil and balsamic vinegar.

Ginger: This not-so-sexy-looking root is oh-so-good for both of you when you eat it. But did you know it also has an effect on you simply by smelling it? That's right, just the scent of ginger might actually increase blood flow to certain parts of his and your bodies. Which part might that be? The genitals. Who knew?

- ⊙ **Recipe Idea**: Try adding fresh ginger to an orange chicken or stir-fry main course. Peel the ginger root and then chop it into chunks or just peel pieces of it right into the pan or wok with the chicken or veggies. It will add a spicy flavor and fantastic fragrance.

Bananas: Perhaps bananas are phallic for a reason...it turns out they can help men's bodies increase their natural production of sex hormones, including testosterone. Bada bing, bada boom!

- ⊙ **Recipe Idea**: Make bananas part of the sweet ending to your sultry dinner. A few hours beforehand, cut the bananas in half and dip them in melted dark chocolate. Freeze them on parchment paper for a delicious dessert.

Flax Seed: Very high in both Omega-3 and Omega-6 fatty acids, flax seed is all the rage in the health-food world. So, what makes it a Blissfully frisky food? Those fatty acids actually play an important role in the body's formation of sex hormones. If your man is getting enough of these, he's likely to have plenty of testosterone, which can boost libido.

- **Recipe Idea:** Try adding flax seed into his morning smoothie to thicken it up or into a healthy muffin recipe.

Declare War on the Snore

If your man's snoring is sabotaging your beauty sleep, there are a few things to consider. First, snoring can be more serious than you might think. If he's consistently snoring, you should nudge him to get to the doctor so they can test him for sleep apnea or other potentially serious medical conditions.

If you've ruled out medical conditions but the snore war rages on, try these tips:

- Realize that the war isn't you against him—it's both of you against the snoring. It's not his fault, so try not to play the blame game. Avoid broaching the subject when you're already both frustrated and tired from lack of sleep.

- Elevate his head by 4 inches using a couple firm, foam pillows.

- Get a humidifier for the bedroom so the air in the room is somewhat humid.

- Put a body pillow behind his back, keeping him on his side while sleeping.

- Encourage him to avoid sleeping pills or alcohol close to bedtime.

- Find a mouth guard online that will keep his mouth in a position that stops the snoring.

· · ·

Yes, there are a lot of man-centric terms and treatments in this chapter, but every one of them works for women, too. Use these ideas and information as opportunities to have fun together, make him feel better, and, in turn, increase your own sexual, romantic, and relationship Bliss.

Chapter 12

Mom Bliss

Moms, I'm amazed that you've made it through even one paragraph of this book while being pulled in at least five directions. (Are you putting the book down right now because the kids just spilled yogurt on the couch?) I'm a mom, and I know firsthand how hard it can be to put yourself first. (Let me guess—you need a second because the little one just fell down?) I get it that you fear taking time for yourself, because everyone depends on you 24/7. (Go ahead and clean up the dog's pee on the carpet before it stains. I'll be here when you get back!) This chapter is especially for you because I understand that sometimes giving yourself permission to focus on and go after your own Bliss sounds like a scene from *Mission Impossible*. I'm with ya, sistah.

You and I both know that motherhood is one of the greatest privileges we can have on this earth. It is the most valuable, important, and amazing job. Raising your children is a heck of a lot of pressure, so it's understandable that we put it above all else. If you're one of the many moms who think that you're doing your kids and family a favor by putting them at the top of a very long list of priorities while you land somewhere between cleaning your car's air-conditioner vent and picking lent off your old sweaters, then I'm happy to tell you that you're very wrong. I believe that it is actually part of our job as being good moms to put ourselves—ready for this?—first on our list of priorities. Yep, I said it. Mom comes first. I am encouraging you to not lose yourself, your desires, your dreams, and your goals because you're too busy running a family and household or because you feel too guilty when you just focus on you for a few minutes each day. Once you get over the guilt, you'll realize that you're actually a more loving and devoted mother, a more relaxed and calm parent, and even a better role model—because your needs have been met.

It's so hard for moms to hear this, and we never say this to each other for fear of sounding like...well, a bad mom! You have needs outside of your family life, and guess what? You have every right to tend to them, not only for your own sake but for the sake of your family. Everyone will be better off, trust me. I'm here to help guide you so that you don't become a martyr who puts herself last for years to come. That won't work for anyone, so it's time to start changing those patterns. Here are some great ways to do just that!

Reconnect the Dots in Your Life

Becoming a mom doesn't mean you stop being a wife, partner, best friend, sister, daughter, colleague, or any of the other hats you wear on a daily basis. Yes, it's the natural tendency for women to take off all other hats and proudly don the mom one most of the time, but if you don't fight that tendency, you can easily get lost. Here are some fun, inexpensive, simple ways to remember what you once loved about yourself if you've forgotten or help you reconnect with the other aspects of yourself that have been on the back burner.

- Wake up 15 minutes earlier or go to bed 15 minutes later every day for five days in a row. Use that time to do whatever brings you Bliss.

  - The options are endless. You might read a fashion or gossip magazine, watch part of your favorite TV show you have saved on the DVR, light candles and hop in a warm tub for a "Calgon, take me away" escape, or express yourself artistically by working on a painting or writing in your journal.

  - There's only one rule: You *must* use this time completely for you, which does not include paying bills, checking email, or dusting the coffee table. I hope you fall so in love with this habit that it becomes permanent!

- Wear that pair of sexy heels currently collecting dust in the back of the closet for no good reason at all. Strut around the house or run your errands in those hot shoes as a reminder that you are a magnificent, dazzling, and desirable woman!

- Call your best friend, sister, or whomever you've blown off one too many times recently because of your schedule or sheer exhaustion. Make a simple plan to meet up ASAP for a cappuccino or a glass of wine. It doesn't have to be anything fancy—you could even have a pajama party in your living room! Just make time with this person to talk, laugh, cry, and connect. Become accountable to this person by sharing that you're making an effort to put yourself first and you want to make this get-together a more regular occurrence.

- If your hubby isn't exactly the type to give you flowers on any day other than Valentine's or your birthday, then leave a flirty note on his computer or in his briefcase and let him know how much you'd love to receive a little bouquet. Remind each other that you're not just "mom," but you're still his wife, and romance matters!

  - Not attached? So what! Order yourself a beautiful arrangement, and every time you look at it, remember that you deserve some recognition for your overall awesomeness. (Yup, I'm making that a word.)

- Do something luxurious for yourself. Even if you have to schedule it a full month in advance (looking forward to a luxury is always fun anyway), find a half-day to go get a massage, facial, body scrub, or spa-style pedicure and just relax. If the price tag seems too high, look online for coupons, or call the spa and ask about any specials they might be running. By being resourceful and flexible on timing, I'll bet you can find a little luxury in your price range.

  - Alternatively, schedule half a day to have the house all to yourself (or with a friend) and do several skin, hair, or body treatments I've recommended without interruption! Play relaxing spa music, wear a fluffy robe, light candles, and nibble on Bliss foods the whole time. I love at-home spa days!

Moms' "I'm Going To" List

Whether you have a two-month old or a house full of teenagers (like I do when Hunter has his friends over), it's valuable to create an "I'm Going To..." list. All too often, this list becomes the "I wish I had" list as years pass, and I don't want that for us. Look, your life doesn't have to stop just because you had kids. You might have to find ways to incorporate kids into your plans, or you might have to beef up childcare now and then to create you time. So, moms, I encourage you to do what it takes, and I promise it will be worth it. OK, stop the steady stream of excuses popping into your head right now, and let your mind go wild. Get creative and journey deep into the crevices of your mind to discover what it is you've wanted to do but you've been endlessly putting off since you became a mom (or longer). Write it down!

1. I'm going to _____

2. I'm going to _____

3. I'm going to _____

   If you need more space, grab a piece of paper and keep on going! Let it all out.

These may not all be things you can accomplish right now, but that doesn't matter. The point of the exercise is just to spend some time getting to know yourself again. You might be surprised by what you find! You're stumped, aren't you? You're not alone. I have a friend who was interviewing moms for a book she was writing. When she asked one, "Aside from your family, what makes you happy?" the woman stared blankly at her. "I'm sorry. Did you say aside from my family?" My friend confirmed what she meant: "Yes. Other than your kids and husband, what brings you joy?" Tears started rolling down the woman's face because she had no idea what else made her happy. She couldn't think of one single thing. I think she cried because she was suddenly met with the harsh reality that she had, indeed, lost some of herself amid the soccer practices, choir performances, doctor appointments, and the millions of details and responsibilities in her life. Sure, she loved her family more than anything and had countless joyful moments with them, but what had she done lately about her own emotional well-being? Zip, zilch, nada. So, let me ask you: What have you done lately for yourself that makes you feel good about who you are? Not much? Well, let's work on that, whatdya say? And if you're still stumped on the "I'm Going To" list, don't worry. Let me help you find it and bring it out.

So Happy Together

Maybe it seems like fun can happen only when there's a babysitter and a bottle of wine involved. Both are great ingredients for a Blissful night, but how about something fun that takes care of your needs while entertaining the kids? If you're in a mom rut, I hope these inexpensive, simple solutions will work great for your family and also stimulate you to think of more ideas on your own.

Wander to a Workshop: Many crafts stores and home-improvement stores feature kid-centric workshops that are fun for Mom too. Do some research online or in your neighborhood to find one that's up your alley—anything from cupcake baking to painting. Alternatively, host a workshop for mom/kid combos. Have everyone bring their own supplies and turn it into a fun get-together.

Throw a Dance Party: A fantastic way to get young kids' wiggles out is to turn on some loud music in the living room and boogie together. Sing out loud, do the twist, and jump around to not only get in some exercise but just to enjoy feeling silly and laughing your heads off.

Plant a Garden: Pick out flowers together at the nursery, and give your kid(s) a special section of your yard to create their very own little garden.

Hone a Talent: If you love to sing, have fun teaching your child your favorite songs, and even plan to put on a private family recital. If writing is more your speed, write a one-act play together and then act it out. Whatever talent or interest you may have, find a way to turn it into a family activity.

Be a Kid Again: What did you love doing when you were a child? What was your favorite game, story, or activity? Take some time to think back to your happiest childhood moments and then re-create them with your own children. Maybe it was an old board game you can find online, or perhaps it was making a tent using a sheet in the living room. I guarantee you'll have fun doing it again and watching the Bliss in your kids' eyes as they experience it for the first time.

A No-Guilt Mom Indulgence:
Kym Brûlée

Who says Crème Brûlée is just for the French or a night out at a fancy restaurant? Now you and your kids can make it right at home and enjoy more than just one bite, since it's super low calorie and low fat. The caramelized crust on top makes it feel oh-so-elegant, so let it inspire a French café evening at home. Play some French music (like the soundtrack to Ratatouille!), light candles, and teach your kids a couple French phrases like "bon appétit!"

Get creative by adding your name or your children's name to the title of any recipe you love like I did. It adds a fun layer of personalization, and who knows, it might even become a family recipe that your great grandkids make someday too!

WHAT YOU NEED

Three 6-ounce cups fat-free Greek yogurt

1 teaspoon vanilla extract (avoid the imitation extract; get the real stuff)

$1/2$ cup preserves (apricot, raspberry, or strawberry are all delicious)

1 tablespoon organic stevia (alternative: 2 tablespoons brown sugar)

2 tablespoons brown sugar (to sprinkle on top)

8 raspberries (or slices of apricot, peach or strawberry)

Yield: 4 servings

WHAT YOU DO

Preheat the broiler in your oven. Mix the stevia and vanilla extract into the Greek yogurt. Cover the bottom of four 4-ounce ramekins with 2 tablespoons of preserves. Top with the fat-free Greek yogurt. Sprinkle the brown sugar on top. Place the ramekins on a baking sheet under broiler until the sugar caramelizes and turns into a crust. Keep a watchful eye so as not to burn them. Let them cool off a little before serving. Place fresh fruit or berry garnish of your choice on top and serve immediately.

Now it's time to open your "I'm Going To..." list and either start writing it or add to it. I'm doing this right along with you and just to inspire you a little, here's my list!

- ◉ Slow dance with Jerry in the living room.
- ◉ Take a long walk on the beach with nothing but my thoughts.
- ◉ Read a book until I fall asleep in the middle of the afternoon.
- ◉ Travel to Scotland and walk the highlands.
- ◉ Plan a girls' weekend.
- ◉ Linger longer at the gym.
- ◉ Drive to Santa Barbara for a day trip with no purpose at all.
- ◉ Take a sewing or knitting class.

If you're still perplexed and can't think of a single thing to put on this list, don't put too much pressure on yourself. Just mull it over for a couple of days, daydream about it, and maybe even do some inspiration research online. Once the flood gates open, you'll suddenly discover a treasure trove of desires hiding in your very soul. Don't be afraid to find them. Instead, embrace them and start laying the groundwork necessary to bring them to Blissful fruition. Maybe not all of them—we have to be realistic here—but one at a time you can start to make headway. I look at it like this: If you never pinpoint that which you really want to do, you have a 0 percent chance of ever doing it. But at least if you know what you want to do, you dramatically increase your odds of actually doing it. Whether it means opening a dedicated savings account for it, enrolling in online courses, or just turning on some music, grabbing your hubby by the hand and forcing him to dance with you in the living room—if you know the goal, you can start doing whatever it takes to achieve it. It doesn't matter how small you start. That savings account can have a $5 balance in it when you open it—that's still a step in the right direction. It's a declarative statement that you have dreams, and you are working toward them.

Listen, if becoming a reality TV star or the next Hollywood sensation is on your list, I have no idea how feasible that really is for you or your family. But I do know that signing up for an acting class is a viable first step. I would never have imagined I'd be a regular guest on Ellen's show, but guess what? My "I'm Going To" list included building a platform to help other women, and now here we are, step-by-step, adding Bliss to our lives together.

Moms, I am one of you. I begged, borrowed, and stole (not literally) to have Hunter, and I thank God every day for the privilege. We have been charged with the mission to care for, mold, and prepare these little humans for everything that life might throw at them. While they're young, we want to create Blissful childhood memories daily for them. But we also have the responsibility of teaching them how to find and experience Bliss on their own. I really like that my teenage son sees me working toward my dreams and doing everything I can to be the best "me" I can be. I hope I'm not only being a role model for him but perhaps also influencing him to seek out a life partner who has a strong sense of self, with clear-cut goals that she's confidently pursuing. I think she will be a stronger partner, friend, and wife to my son than a woman who stands in the shadows, only existing to please others. Not that I get a vote!

. . .

Their childhood flashes by in a moment, and we as moms can't follow them around making sure they're happy all the time. But starting right now, we can set a wonderful example for them by taking excellent care of ourselves and our own happiness. What have you done for your own Bliss lately that will inspire your children?

Chapter 13

Pet Bliss

Have you ever looked at your pet and tried to imagine what you'd see if Fido had a thought bubble over his head? If I had to guess what the thought bubbles over my golden retriever Brady's head said, it'd go something like this: "Oh, yay, Mom's home. Did she bring me food? I'm so excited I could pee! But I know I shouldn't. Oh, she's petting me. A little to the left! Don't forget my butt—you know how I love my butt to be scratched. And, wait! Is that food I smell? Food! Oops, I peed a little. Sorry, Mom!" That pretty much sums up his internal monologue on a daily basis, at least how I imagine it. My family and I don't just love Brady—he plays a critical role in our overall Bliss (despite his occasional "accidents" on the floor!).

If you're a pet lover, you know how it feels when your dog, cat, parakeet, hamster, or any other animal with whom you have formed a bond looks at you with that deep, unconditional look of love in his eyes. There's really nothing like it! They depend on you completely, and they show their appreciation for every little thing you do for them, probably unlike anyone else in your life. So, this chapter is devoted to some of the ways you can improve your relationship with your pet so you can increase your Bliss Factor. But, guys, let me tell you without making an apology—I am a dog person. That's just me! Naturally, I'm not saying you can't have cat Bliss or whatever animal you choose, but I'm just not the right gal to tell you how because I am all about big, furry pups, so my advice is geared toward dog lovers. Modify it any way you need to, OK?

The Greatest Gatsby

I'd like to share with you the story of how we came to own our first dog. Jerry and I had been trying for five years to have a baby. It was a tumultuous and emotional journey, and we were both starting to feel our Bliss slip out of our grasp. We thought we could temporarily fill the hole in our hearts by adopting a dog. And the moment we laid eyes on this blockhead golden retriever (that's actually the type of golden he was, and true to the name, his head was approximately the size of a large filing cabinet), we knew we'd made the right decision. I was enamored with *The Great Gatsby*, and I swear this dog bore a beautiful resemblance to Robert Redford, so we named him Gatsby. He was my first baby.

I was pregnant with Hunter a year after adopting Gatsby—and I really think it's thanks to the amazing way he loved us, calmed us down, and taught us to take things in stride. Hunter's first word was even "Ga" instead of "Ma" or "Pa"—yep, that dog was just as much a part of the family as any of us. Since then, we've never been without a dog—sometimes three—in the house. It's just amazing how much pets enrich your Bliss, isn't it?

Hairy Situations

As soft and cuddly as our furry critters are, sometimes all that fur just feels like it's taking over the house! Hairballs gather along the floorboards, and fur gets stuck to our clothes, furniture, and even pillows. Here is a surefire way to approach your pet's hairy situations around your home.

Pet Bliss Treatment #1:
Fight Fur with Rubber

WHAT YOU NEED

Latex gloves

Water

Fur, as you know, seems to stick to everything, but it sticks surprisingly well to rubber. Use this to your advantage with this quick fur fix. I do this right before we have company over, and it works like a charm so no one's pants are covered in Brady's fur when they stand up.

WHAT YOU DO

Put the gloves on your hands and get them slightly wet. Then rub your gloved hands all over the affected furniture. You'll notice lots of pet hair sticking to them, but some of it might just clump up together, so just pick up the clumps and throw them away. *Voila!*

Smelly Dog

I know the song on *Friends* was actually "Smelly Cat," but in reality, dogs tend to be the smelly ones. Cats usually take great Bliss in obsessively cleaning themselves, but dogs, well, let's just say hygiene isn't their number-one concern in life. Giving your dog a bath on a daily basis isn't good for his skin or your schedule, so here are a couple ways to help quell the smell.

Pet Bliss Treatment #2:
Dry Shampoo for Fido

WHAT YOU NEED

1 box of baking soda

1 smelly dog

Baking soda is a natural deodorizer that removes bad smells in your refrigerator, but it can also work wonders on your dog!

WHAT YOU DO

Take your dog in the backyard so you don't get baking soda everywhere in your house. Sprinkle the baking soda liberally on the fur. Then rub it in with your hands and run a brush through to really work it in. This will soak up the nasty smells and give your dog a fresh scent.

Pet Bliss Treatment #3:
The Stink-No-More Bath

WHAT YOU NEED

2 cups plain oatmeal

2 cotton balls

Room temperature water

Outdoor basin or indoor bathtub

When you can literally smell your dog coming down the hall, it might be time for a special bath. Resist the urge to reach for heavily fragranced human shampoo or conditioner—they aren't great for dogs' coats or skin. Instead, go *au natural* with this oatmeal bath, which will help remove dander and dirt from his coat and also absorb odors.

WHAT YOU DO

If you're doing this procedure in a bathtub, you'll want to put something on the drain so it won't let the oatmeal go through—an upside-down strainer over the drain works well.

Put the oatmeal in a food processor or blender until it is a powder. Mix water with it until it's a paste. Gently place the cotton balls at the opening of your dog's ears so that water doesn't get inside the ear canal. (Or just be careful to avoid the ears as you bathe him.) Wet his coat completely with cool water until completely saturated. Take the oatmeal mixture into your hands and rub it into the fur on your dog's back, belly, and legs. Avoid scrubbing, because you might irritate his skin. If you can keep your dog from running off and rolling in the grass or dirt, try to keep the mixture on for at least five minutes.

Then, thoroughly rinse it all off with cool water because dogs naturally have a higher body temperature than humans, and you don't want to overheat them with warm or hot water. Pat him dry or use a blow-dryer on the cool setting because the hot air can irritate the skin and overheat your pup. Now he's clean as a whistle, which inevitably means he's just moments away from seeking out all manner of dirt and grime to roll around in. That's just the nature of this sweet beast!

Is Your Dog Socially Awkward?

We recently went out of town and wanted to leave Brady at a dog hotel rather than the usual kennel. This isn't as simple a proposition as you might assume. Apparently they have to determine whether each dog checking into the doggy hotel for the weekend is properly socialized and able to play well with others. (This is Hollywood after all, so your own social standing, your kids' social standing, and your nanny's social standing are insufficient ways of judging someone. Your dog must also be in excellent social standing—crazy!) Well, we agreed to have him tested. I was on pins and needles the whole time, hopeful that he'd perform well and make me proud (and not lose his head and bark rudely at someone!). Alas, he made the cut—they pronounced him highly social. What a relief! He apparently took a particular liking to a hot little French poodle and a chocolate labradoodle. What can I say? He has great taste. We checked him into the posh dog hotel, where he got to laze around on his very own bed, watch TV, and have a vacation of his very own. No kidding, I think his vacay cost more than ours, but he deserved a little spoiling.

Love Doesn't Hurt

I sincerely hope this goes without saying, but no matter how frustrated you might get with your pet after he pees on the carpet for the one billionth time or barks at every sound or movement, please never, ever strike your dog. Not only will hitting, spanking, or swatting your dog make him afraid of you (and steal his Bliss away), it will also make training impossible because it's all about building and maintaining trust between you and your dog. If you hit him, you'll lose his trust. Got that? Good; moving on!

If your dog is less than socially acceptable to his canine peers (and your family), you definitely have options. Now, before I delve into this too deeply, let me be clear. Brady isn't exactly the picture of perfect pet behavior, and I'm a far cry from being a dog trainer, whisperer, or expert. But these are some simple techniques I've researched and found to work when used properly. Give them a try, but obviously if your pet is putting you or your family in danger or making your life consistently miserable with his bad behavior, by all means, seek the assistance and advice of a professional!

Sit. Stay. Good Dog.

It can be tough to have a Blissful home life when one family member—not naming any names, but perhaps it's the four-legged one—isn't following instructions and has the whole family at their wit's end. You might be thinking, "I'm going to train my dog once and for all." If there's ever a statement that falls under the category of "easier said than done," this is right up there with "I'm going to lose 30 pounds." Obedience training your dog is an undertaking that, first and foremost, requires patience on your part. Your dog wants to do right by you, even if sometimes it seems like all he wants to do is pee on the carpet and bark his head off, so you have to show him when he does something right. The following are some tried-and-true techniques that have worked for me. If these don't apply to your particular canine conundrums, I suggest you do as much homework as you can before giving in to the mayhem. There are tons of online resources and videos with great info on how to train your dog on your own as well as local trainers who can lend you a hand. The point is to persevere and be consistent, and eventually your dog will reward you by asking to go outside rather than leaving a puddle by the door. Also, keep in mind that a training technique that works like a charm for one dog may not work as perfectly for another dog. Just like humans, they all have personalities and even baggage, so teaching obedience is not a one-size-fits-all kind of thing. But keep working on it, and the two of you will soon start to understand each other.

Is This Dog Deaf or What?

We all probably have someone in our life that occasionally suffers from selective hearing. OK, maybe your teenager is just ignoring you when you ask him for the ten-thousandth time to pick up his dirty socks from the living room floor because he's currently more engaged in the video game he's playing. Similarly, when your dog is nose deep in a particularly fragrant (or urine-soaked) patch of grass, the last thing he wants to do is come running when you call his name. It's sort of against his instinct. But it is possible, with training, to improve his recall abilities. And this is super important because it could save his life someday! If you've ever learned how to ski, you know the very first thing the instructors teach you is how to stop. There's nothing more dangerous than a beginner skier rocketing down the mountain without knowing how to put on the brakes. Similarly, should your dog get loose in an area with any traffic, you definitely want it engrained in his brain to come back to you when you call.

Pet Bliss Treatment #4:
Tips for Total Doggy Recall

WHAT YOU NEED

Handful of dog treats

Long training leash (approximately 20 feet)

WHAT YOU DO

This is a great activity to get the family involved in because you'll need some assistance. Plus, it's important that everyone who typically interacts with the dog is on the same page about commands so he doesn't get confused. Put the long leash on the dog and walk away from him, holding the end of the leash. Make sure he hasn't eaten recently so he's particularly interested in the treats. Have someone gently hold him so he can't run to you until you're ready.

Wait until he's sitting and relatively calm, and also make sure you and your assistant are calm and confident. Your dog picks up on your energy very easily, so if you're nervous and unsure, he will be too. Then, hold a treat up and say, "Come!" The assistant should immediately let go of the dog who will (ideally) come running to you. Immediately reward him by saying "Yes!" and giving him the treat and a good rub. You've just rewarded him for good behavior, thus reinforcing it as such in his mind. Repeat this process for a total of about 20 repetitions, which is usually less than 10 minutes, and then stop for the day so you don't wear him out and he doesn't start to get distracted. Also, working in these short bursts not only makes it more realistic for your schedule but keeps the dog in the mind-set of "playtime" instead of work. Ideally, you should make time for training every day to get the fastest results. This should really be a fun bonding time for everyone, including your dog.

TIP: Carry little pieces of dog treats or oat cereal in your pocket around the house, and when the dog is lounging around in another room, call his name. When he arrives at your side, immediately give him the tiny treat. This way, you're constantly reinforcing the training.

Good Dog, Bad Human

So many dog owners (yes, me included) unknowingly punish our pups when they actually do something good! For instance, on the rare occasion that your dog actually does come to you when you call, are you immediately putting them in a bathtub, clamping a leash on them, or yelling because of something they did five minutes ago? In all of those cases, you've just inadvertently communicated "bad dog" right after they've done something good. You have to think of everything with your dog as either a punishment or a reward and realize that your dog lives in the present. They don't remember what they did five minutes ago, but they do remember what they did five seconds ago. Live in the now with your dog, and reward or punish them based on that.

To Pee or Not to Pee...on the Carpet

If your dog spends the majority of his time indoors with the family, you'll want him to learn how to mind his potty manners. Just because he's the only four-legged family member doesn't mean he gets to relieve himself on the floor. Housetraining is possible, though I know how it is to have a dog who pees every time he gets excited about something. Oh, Brady. I've thought many times about just putting a diaper on him. Here are some important rules that, when followed consistently, can go a long way toward keeping urination nation outdoors!

Pet Bliss Treatment #5:
Housetraining Know-How

- Puppies can't hold it for very long, so take him out at least every two hours if he's very young.

- Make peeing a priority in his mind. When you take him out, tell him to "go pee pee" first and then reward him with a treat. Then take him to enjoy some playtime or a walk.

- Make a schedule and stick with it. If you're feeding him at the same time daily, he'll have to go potty around the same time, and you'll quickly instill a consistent routine where he knows what is expected of him.

- If yellow stains seem to magically appear every morning, try picking up the water bowl one or two hours before bedtime so his bladder isn't full at night.

- Keep a watchful eye and learn his pre-pee signs. If he's sniffing around the carpet, scratching at the door, or circling frantically, he's probably about to let 'er rip. When you spot the behavior, let him outside and reward him when he goes in the grass.

Turn Down the Volume on Your Woofer

Whether your dog has a tiny, squeaky yap or a big, deep, scary sounding woof, incessant barking can surely affect everyone's ability to have Bliss in your household. Just like you learn how to interpret a child's cry (the poop cry vs. the hunger cry, and so on), it's smart to learn how to interpret your dog's barks, growls, howls, and whines. Remember when I was saying earlier that you shouldn't reward the dog when he's done something wrong? That applies in the case of nonstop barking too—be careful or you risk teaching the dog that it's socially acceptable for him to bark his head off for no good reason. Just like with any type of obedience training, teaching a dog not to bark out of boredom or curiosity takes patience and perseverance. You can do it, though!

Pet Bliss Treatment #6:
Less Bark for Your Buck

Here are some guidelines to help show your dog that you're the conversationalist in the family, not him! A bark by the door to remind you to let him out or the greeting when you come home from a long day is perfectly fine, but that's it.

- ⊙ Wear your dog out with healthy play.

  Just like with kids, the more tired your dog is, the less likely he is to get into trouble, including barking hysterically.

- ⊙ When he raises the volume, don't match him by yelling.

  He barks, you yell, and suddenly it's just a big, fun game to him. Resist the urge to scream.

- ⊙ Punish by ignoring.

  When he's barking and wanting attention, if you do the opposite and just turn your back, he'll eventually pipe down.

- ⊙ Teach the "quiet" command.

  Yes, there's a "quiet" command! When he's barking, calmly say "shh," and then hold a treat in front of his nose. He'll stop barking to sniff it (thus, he'll go quiet), and then he'll eat it. Tell him he's a good dog and give him a pet. When he barks again, repeat the process. Keep rewarding him every time he quiets down at the command. Have treats on hand all the time during the training process!

. . .

Pets are just as much part of the family as the human family members, but everyone's relationship with their pet is unique. Some of my friends let their dogs sleep right up on the pillows with them, and others wouldn't dream of allowing their pets in the house, much less on the furniture. As long as the relationship is healthy and safe for all parties involved, it can be one of our most rewarding and Blissful relationships in your lives.

Chapter 14

Living Bliss Plan

Reading about Bliss is definitely a step in the right direction, but there's still work ahead if you're going to really start living Blissfully, so let's get to it. The goal of this week is to get you prepared for the Blissful habits you'll form during the 30-day Bliss Plan. Think of this week as a time to delve into what does and, just as importantly, does not bring you Bliss. This is a chance to make assessments of different areas your life, from your environment to your moods, energy, and the many roles you play. This is your chance to wake up and stop the tendency to get through the day like a zombie, whether that's because you're exhausted all the time or because you're living on auto-pilot. You'll learn how to put up your Bliss radar, and once you have pinpointed your Bliss, you can protect it and even project it to others. And when you have figured out the things that steal your Bliss, you can steer clear of them or fix them. Let's start by going over the guidelines that apply to each day.

Living Bliss Deal-Breakers

A few things apply to every day of this one-week routine. Don't just gloss over these, dolls, because following these principles on a daily basis will go a long way toward increasing your Bliss Factor.

Daily Must-Haves

- ⊙ You've started some wonderful habits with the Beauty Bliss Plan, especially in the area of your diet and exercise. Please keep 'em up

  - ▢ Eat *Bliss Foods* (on page 80) while avoiding *Debbie Downer Foods* (on page 87).

  - ▢ Drink plenty of water to keep that skin gorgeous.

  - ▢ Do *Bliss-ercise* for at least 22 minutes each day.

  - ▢ Enjoy your *Rise 'n' Shine Minty Lime* drink (recipe on page 88) every morning as soon as you wake up, preferably instead of coffee.

- ⊙ Incorporate one cup of chamomile or green tea into your daily routine for a natural energy boost.

- ⊙ Go "shopping" in your own closet and pick out a few new outfit combinations that will bring you Bliss. Take a look at the *Bliss-Dressed List* on page 128 for some ideas on ideal colors to choose.

Ready? Great, because Day 1 starts right now!

Day 1

Today's Date: _____

Upon waking, enjoy your *Rise 'n' Shine Minty Lime* drink (recipe on page 88) instead of coffee.

Write your number-one living Bliss goal for this week. (Remember: Push yourself, but also be realistic.) _____

Stay aware of your energy level throughout the day. Is your energy low, moderate, or high?

Time of Day: Energy Level:

Morning: _____

Midday: _____

Evening: _____

Take inventory of the following physical areas of your life and rate them on a scale of 1 to 10, with 1 being Bliss kryptonite and 10 being sheer Bliss. It might help if you physically go into the space and write down the first score that pops in your head.

Space: Score:

Living room   _____

Bedroom   _____

Kitchen   _____

Home office   _____

Closets   _____

Bathroom   _____

Kids' rooms   _____

Car   _____

Based on these numbers, you know which areas you need to focus on the most over the course of this week and the 30-day Bliss Plan. Don't stress even if you rated every area as a 1 because the subtlest of changes can clear clutter and help make a dent in bringing a little (or a lot) of Bliss into your home.

Start by tackling the biggest problem in the room that you rated lowest. (If there's more than one room with the same low score, pick either—ultimately they both have to become Blissful.) Spend 22 minutes focused on doing whatever is necessary to get the room up to at least an 8 (though ideally a 10). Why 22 minutes? If you aim for spending 22 minutes, you're giving yourself a more realistic goal, and you're more likely to use every minute of it accomplishing the task.

Space: _____

Issues:_____

If 22 minutes are up and you love the progress and want to continue, go for it. But if your back is aching and you're ready to call it a day, then do exactly that and be extremely proud of what you got done. Here are some examples to give you the gist:

- If your laundry is spilling out of the hamper or scattered around the bedroom, spend the time folding, hanging, and putting away the clothes.

  Tip: Put on high-energy dance music so you can move and groove as you fluff and fold.

- If your problem is paperwork piled up in an office space, sort through as many piles as you can, and put the papers into properly labeled boxes or a file system. Not everything has to be handled, but you do need to at least create some semblance of organization in the 22 minutes that you've allotted.

- If your car looks like a tornado ripped through it, throw away the trash or organize the glove box.

  Tip: If there's a self-serve car wash near your home, take it there so you can vacuum out the crumbs as you chuck the junk.

- If clutter isn't your issue or isn't the only issue, then try to identify the other problems with the room or space. Again, pinpointing a problem is the first step to solving it.

Turn to pages 117–118 to find out *Interior Bliss Tips* if you're past the clutter and on to feathering your nest.

End of day: Record one or two things that happened today that made you feel Blissful. These can be fleeting moments that made you smile or day-long activities that filled your heart with happiness.

Today I felt Bliss when: _____

_____

_____

Day 2

Today's Date: _____

Upon waking, enjoy your *Rise 'n' Shine Minty Lime* drink (recipe on page 88) instead of coffee.

Perform 10 minutes of yoga poses (you'll find a list of my favorites on page 139) in a quiet place in your home. This simple exercise will set a calm yet energetic tone for your entire day.

Stay aware of your energy level throughout the day. Is your energy low, moderate, or high? Keep tabs on this every day this week, knowing that you can't fix it all right this minute but acknowledging when you sink vs. when you're energized is the first step toward making positive changes, which you will surely do in the 30-day Bliss Plan!

Time of Day: Energy Level:

Morning: _____

Midday: _____

Evening: _____

Think about the ways certain people in your life rob you of your Bliss. Now, think about creative ways you can combat that negativity. Some examples include a friend you have a long history with so you stay in each other's lives, but all she does is complain, or a co-worker who somehow decided you're his go-to for all his whining about the workplace when, in fact, you like your job. Obviously, you cannot control other people's actions and words, but you can limit your involvement with them and/or control how you respond and how you let it affect you.

How others sometimes rob me of Bliss: _____

_____

_____

Ways I can combat the negativity and project Bliss: _____

_____

_____

Spend 22 minutes cutting the clutter, organizing or beautifying another space you rated Bliss-less or close to it.

Today I felt Bliss when: _____

_____

_____

Day 3

Today's Date: _____

Upon waking, enjoy your *Rise 'n' Shine Minty Lime* drink (recipe on page 88) instead of coffee.

If you're a mom, think of one thing you can do this week to reconnect with yourself. Check out the ideas under *Reconnect the Dots in Your Life* on page 164 for inspiration.

Stay aware of your energy level throughout the day. Is your energy low, moderate, or high?

Time of Day:	Energy Level:
Morning:	_____
Midday:	_____
Evening:	_____

Spend 22 minutes cutting the clutter, organizing, or beautifying a space you rated Bliss-less or close to it. (Note: You have the option this week of continuing in one space each day or switching between several areas. You don't want to get bogged down, so if you get sick of one room, start working on another one.)

Today I felt Bliss when: _____

_____

_____

Day 4

Today's Date: _____

Upon waking, enjoy your *Rise 'n' Shine Minty Lime* drink (recipe on page 88) instead of coffee.

Take 7 to 10 minutes before starting your day to just be with yourself. Maybe spend this time meditating silently, watching your favorite TV show saved on the DVR, or reading a gossip magazine. This may mean setting the alarm a few minutes earlier so you have complete peace (no kids screaming your name, and so on), but it's worth it.

If there's a man in your life who needs some treatments, pick one that I mentioned in Chapter 11, "Man Bliss." Give him a head's up about how fun it'll be for both of you!

Stay aware of your energy level throughout the day. Is your energy low, moderate, or high?

Time of Day: Energy Level:

Morning: _____

Midday: _____

Evening: _____

Spend 22 minutes cutting the clutter, organizing, or beautifying another space you rated Bliss-less or close to it.

Today I felt Bliss when: _____

_____

_____

Day 5

Today's Date: _____

Upon waking, enjoy your *Rise 'n' Shine Minty Lime* drink (recipe on page 88) instead of coffee.

Think about three specific ways you're going to give Bliss away to someone else today. These can be small gestures to strangers or big favors to friends or family members. Write them here, and do your best to fit all three in today.

I will give Bliss by: _____

I will give Bliss by: _____

I will give Bliss by: _____

Stay aware of your energy level throughout the day. Is your energy low, moderate, or high?

Time of Day: Energy Level:

Morning: _____

Midday: _____

Evening: _____

Spend 22 minutes cutting the clutter, organizing, or beautifying another space you rated Bliss-less or close to it.

Today I felt Bliss when: _____

_____

_____

Day 6

Today's Date: _____

Upon waking, enjoy your *Rise 'n' Shine Minty Lime* drink (recipe on page 88) instead of coffee.

Stay aware of your energy level throughout the day. Is your energy low, moderate, or high?

Time of Day: Energy Level:

Morning: _____

Midday: _____

Evening: _____

Since the week is almost over and I don't know anyone who gets through a week without at least one energy slump, I think this is a great day to get the ingredients and make a few *DIY Blissful Energy Bars* (recipe on page 136) to have on hand.

Spend 22 minutes cutting the clutter, organizing, or beautifying another space you rated Bliss-less or close to it.

Today I felt Bliss when: _____

_____

_____

Day 7

Today's Date: _____

Upon waking, enjoy your *Rise 'n' Shine Minty Lime* drink (recipe on page 88) instead of coffee.

Perform ten minutes of yoga poses, concentrating on contracting your tummy muscles and breathing deeply. Today, make a conscious effort to stand up straighter by using strength from your core, and exude confidence because you are a beautiful, smart, loving, powerful woman. Got that?

Stay aware of your energy level throughout the day. Is your energy low, moderate, or high?

Time of Day: Energy Level:
Morning: _____
Midday: _____
Evening: _____

Spend 22 minutes cutting the clutter, organizing, or beautifying another space you rated Bliss-less or close to it.

Today I felt Bliss when: _____

_____

Write down the positive changes you've made this week. Have you made some headway with the clutter in your various environments? Do you have a better sense of your fluctuating energy levels? Are you more aware of what makes you Blissful and what doesn't so you can start making adjustments? All of those things are amazing progress. Write down any changes, big or small, and record them here.

Positive Changes: _____

_____

Congratulations! You've done a fantastic job laying the ground-work for Bliss in your life. Think of this past week as just a little taste of what's in store for you in the next 30 days. Now is when you begin incorporating Bliss into every facet of your life. Are you ready for the main course? It's called the Bliss Plan, and it's yours for the taking. Take a deep breath, acknowledge the hard work you've already put in, and let's do this!

Part 4

The Bliss Plan

OK, ladies, it's true that Bliss happens, but only if you help make it happen! So, it's time to put my Bliss Plan into action. This 30-day plan brings my philosophies on beauty, living, and inexpensive, simple solutions together and breaks them down into daily tasks. Don't worry, they're not really "tasks" because none of this should feel like a task—quite the contrary—but I am recognizing that in the beginning you may wonder how you'll find the time to change your patterns and make these activities a priority. The answer is that you simply will, because 30 days from now you will be reaping huge rewards that can last you for a lifetime. You're making a serious investment in your happiness—pardon the soap-opera references, but you have only "one life to live," so why not make it a Blissful, "young and the restless" (or in this case, young and well-rested!) one?

Before you start, I urge you to go all the way back to the Bliss Quiz you took at the very beginning of this book. When you look closely at your answers, certain areas of your life will show that they need more attention than others. Keep that in mind as you embark upon the next 30 days. Are you a mom who desperately needs to reconnect with yourself? Is your chaotic home environment stealing your Bliss? Do you avoid mirrors at all costs because you aren't investing enough time and effort into your health, beauty, and body? If your most dire Bliss fixes fall into one category, obviously that's where you'll need to invest more of your energy during the next 30 days. I am about to spell it all out for you, but of course you can tailor the plan to your life and needs. This is not a one-size-fits-all solution (well, maybe one-size-fits-most, or else I wouldn't be so sure that you're going to succeed).

I'm not so Pollyanna-ish as to suggest that if you follow this plan, suddenly you'll be skipping through the streets and everything will fall perfectly into place in your life. You and I both know that life can be overwhelming—sh*% happens, but so do Blissful things if we make them. So, for the next month, let's focus on all that we can have control over, which I hope you've realized by now is quite a lot.

One of the most important directives I have for you over the next month is to find the humor in pretty much everything. Life is better when you're laughing, so laugh when you'd rather scream, and smile when you'd rather pout. It's easier said than done when something is frustrating you to no end, but just that simple switch will change things more than you might know.

Chapter 15

The 30-Day Bliss Plan

I wholeheartedly believe that if you want to discover Bliss in your life, this is where you should start. First and foremost I want to make sure you know that this 30-day plan is doable. Yes, even for you! I've designed it with extraordinarily busy women in mind (I don't know any other kind of woman!), so I believe the time commitment is manageable. Yes, you might need to juggle your schedule a bit more than you already do to fit these things in, but that's part of the point—to learn how to make time to do the things that will boost your Bliss. I'm not exactly telling you to take leave from your life and go spend a month at a retreat, for goodness sake!

Of course, there will be those crazy days when you can hardly keep your head above water, much less get into the fantasy at-home sauna for 20 minutes to meditate in silence. When that happens, it's up to you to tone down the plan accordingly.

Conversely, if you're so gung-ho that you want to dedicate extra attention to your "Bliss-ification," by all means, do so. A little "extra credit" work on your skin, hair, body, environment, energy, or inner Bliss can only work in your favor.

Some of the activities in this plan will be brand new for you and may be out of your comfort zone. If you're one of those women who is always running around doing things for others, the idea of taking even just a few minutes in the morning or at night to focus on your own Bliss may be earth-shattering for you! Other activities have, I hope, already become familiar to you over the past two weeks, and now it's about maintaining those habits for the next 30 days.

I know I've said it before, but it bears repeating as you begin these transformative 30 days. I'm not a doctor, nutritionist, psychologist, or any other expert along those lines. But I have worked hard at my own Bliss, and I've seen how countless other women have had success. Be smart about changing your habits, girls, and have a chat with your physician if you have any questions or concerns. And now... onward and upward, Bliss soldiers!

Bliss Must-Haves

Here's your list of daily must-haves for your next 30 days. These are simple concepts, but they're vital to this overall plan.

- Think about the foods you're choosing to eat. Ask yourself before each meal, snack, or random bite (yes, those count!) whether that food will contribute to your health and therefore your Bliss or whether it will sabotage both. Here are some ways to keep you on track:

    - Wherever you go during the day, whether it's to an office, driving kids around, errands, or anywhere else life might take you, bring healthy snacks with you and/or pack your lunch.

- ☐ Choose *Bliss Foods* (on page 80) or mostly whole, natural foods such as fruits, veggies, and light proteins.

- ☐ If you're a junk food junkie, get rid of all those fatty, salty, greasy bagged, boxed, or packaged foods in your cupboard before you even start this monthlong Bliss mission.

- ☐ If you're an aficionado of fine drive-thru cuisine, I encourage you to give it up, cold turkey, for the next 30 days. Replace those afternoon French fry indulgences with a more nutritious alternative. I get it. If you're a mom and there's really no way around hitting up the drive-thru after your kids' grueling soccer, football, or baseball practice, then find something healthy on the menu for yourself: a salad, fruit, or grilled chicken are great options. I know when I take Hunter to In-N-Out Burger, I'll just order a protein-style burger (lettuce wrapped instead of a bun). Yum!

- ☐ Keep plenty of water on hand so you can more easily avoid the temptation to guzzle soda (diet or otherwise). Do you know what's in the fountain of youth? Water! Drink it!

- ◉ Moms especially, but this applies to everyone: Work on an "I'm Going To" List (examples on page 166) at least twice a week during this month.

- ◉ Take note of your energy patterns you tracked during the Living Bliss Plan.

  - ☐ Every day this month, make a conscious effort about an hour before your typical energy slump to perform the *Energy Bliss Treatment* (on pages 135–141) that most applies to you. Soon you'll be staving off all your comatose moments throughout the day and slowly morph into your own version of the Energizer Bunny.

- ◉ Get serious about your sleep habits this month. In Chapter 10, "Energy Bliss," review how to *Adopt a Pre-sleep Ritual*, and try your best to do this each night for the next 30 days. You will be shocked by what a consistent sleep schedule will do for your Bliss Factor, you guys!

◉ When you're staring into your closet each morning trying to decide what to wear, make a conscious effort to choose an outfit that will inspire you, make you stand up straight, and exude confidence. Take a look at the *Bliss-Dressed List* on page 128 for some suggestions on ideal colors to choose. Trust me, this matters, and it can make a big difference in your day.

◉ I also want you to gauge your daily Bliss, focusing on even the littlest things that make you happy.

　　◻ Maybe it's the gentle sound of the dishwasher doing work for you, a compliment from someone at work, or the look in your child's face when you're reading him a bedtime story.

　　◻ Find something to be Blissful about and write it down because the more you acknowledge Bliss, in all its forms, the more you'll feel it and draw it to you.

◉ There are days in this plan in which you'll be dedicating a total of about an hour to your Bliss throughout the day, at times that work well for you. At first glance, that may seem like more time than you can carve out, but keep in mind that it's worth it! We're talking about little pockets of time throughout the day, and the payoff will be huge. Do your best, but the goal here is not to be hard on yourself if you just can't make everything jive with your schedule. All I ask is that if you can't quite get to everything on the Plan on certain days, don't, under any circumstances, beat yourself up. Just pick right back up the next day and continue toward your Bliss. Got it?

NOTE: You'll see an asterisk next to the "optional" tasks. These are specifically designed for moms or pet owners. Just ignore 'em if they don't apply to you.

Day 1

Today's Date: _____

How will you give Bliss away today? Get creative! Examples: Tell the barista at your coffee shop that she's doing a good job, hold the door open for a woman with a stroller who is struggling to do it on her own, write a note to your hubby telling him one thing you adore about him, or say "thank you" to a serviceman or woman who you see. _____

_____

_____

Do 22 minutes of *Bliss-ercise* or regular exercise today. (Examples on page 90.)

Perform a skin treatment (in Chapter 3, "Skin Bliss") that is most applicable to your needs.

*Moms: Make some time today for bonding with your kids while feeling entertained yourself. Refer to the *So Happy Together* list on page 167 for a few ideas. This can be just a few minutes or longer, depending on your schedule.

Spend 22 minutes decluttering, organizing, or beautifying one of your environments like your closet, office, car, or bedroom. Follow the guidelines in Chapter 9, "Environment Bliss."

For dinner, include some Blissfully Frisky Foods (on page 159). These will rev up your (and his) engine, but even if that's not your goal, they're great for your overall health.

Today I felt Bliss when: _____

_____

_____

Day 2

Today's Date: _____

Do 22 minutes of *Bliss-ercise* or regular exercise today. (Examples on page 90.)

Perform a hair treatment (in Chapter 5, "Hair Bliss") that is most suited to your hair needs.

Make a batch of your favorite *DIY Blissful Energy Bars* (on page 136) and nosh on them about an hour before your energy typically begins to wane (based on the data you collected during the Living Bliss Plan).

*Pet owners: If your pet is due for a Pet Bliss treatment (found in Chapter 13, "Pet Bliss"), today is the day! Your pet will love the extra attention!

Write down five things you are grateful for in your life. The next time a negative thought tries to get a foothold in your mind, take a look at this list.

_____

_____

_____

_____

_____

Today I felt Bliss when: _____

_____

_____

Day 3

Today's Date: _____

Start off the day with a *Dandelion Bloat-Buster Tea* (recipe on page 95) ideally instead of coffee.

Do 22 minutes of *Bliss-ercise* or regular exercise today. (Examples on page 90.)

Which nail treatment (in Chapter 6, "Nails Bliss") do you most need? Make it happen today.

Spend 22 minutes decluttering, organizing, or beautifying one of your environments.

Have fun doing a Man Bliss treatment (on pages 148–159) on your guy. Your pick (or maybe his).

Today I felt Bliss when: _____

_____

_____

Day 4

Today's Date: _____

Do 22 minutes of *Bliss-ercise* or regular exercise today. (Examples on page 90.)

Perform a face treatment (in Chapter 4, "Face Bliss") that best suits your needs.

Think about something that inspires you. Maybe it's the lyrics to a song or something a celebrity said in an interview about rising to stardom out of absolutely nothing. Write it down (on a sticky note, in your smartphone, anywhere!) and let it motivate you to keep going strong throughout this month.

_____

_____

Find seven minutes today to be completely quite. Turn off all the electronics and focus on your inner voice. Write down where your thoughts take you. _____

_____

_____

Today I felt Bliss when: _____

_____

_____

Day 5

Today's Date: _____

Write down the two most common excuses you make for not taking the best possible care of yourself. (Some common ones I hear: "I'm too tired to get up early for exercise" or " I don't have time to perform beauty treatments on myself.")

_____

_____

Now, write what you will do instead when you try to use these tired old excuses over the next 25 days. (For example, "If I just force myself out of bed, I'll feel energized for the rest of the day." Or, "I'll make the time because my Bliss matters.")

_____

_____

Do 22 minutes of *Bliss-ercise* or regular exercise today. (Examples on page 90.)

Spend 22 minutes focusing on making your bedroom a relaxing, peaceful sanctuary. This could mean spraying lavender water on the pillows, putting fresh flowers in vases on your bedside table, removing some clutter, folding laundry, or any other task. The end goal is to make this room the perfect environment for Blissful rest, and 22 minutes will sure make a dent.

Today I felt Bliss when: _____

_____

_____

Day 6

Is there a deep desire has your inner voice been telling you that you've been ignoring? Spend no more than 30 seconds thinking about it and then write the first thing that comes to mind, even if it's completely outlandish.

_____

_____

Become aware of your inner voice over the rest of the Bliss Plan and start to think about ways you can achieve whatever it's telling you.

Have a *Dandelion Bloat-Buster Tea* (recipe on page 95) this afternoon with a light snack.

Do 22 minutes of *Bliss-ercise* or regular exercise. (Examples on page 90.)

No bad-hair day for you today! Pick a hair treatment (from Chapter 5, "Hair Bliss") to perform today.

Today I felt Bliss when: _____

_____

_____

Day 7

Today's Date: _____

Choose two people in your life who have done something recently for which they wouldn't expect to receive a handwritten thank-you note, and send them one anyway. I love picking out cute little cards and surprising friends with a heartfelt note. It just takes a couple minutes of your time and the cost of a stamp, but you'll receive such Bliss from it!

No *Bliss-ercise* or exercise required today—it's your rest day.

Perform a body treatment (in Chapter 7, "Body Bliss") that will most benefit you.

Pick one section of your closet to clean out. Maybe it's just your collection of jeans or your stash of T-shirts. Separate the clothes into three piles: keep, give away, and trash. Spend 22 minutes on this task, and if this is the last thing on Earth you want to do, change your perception of it by turning on fun music or getting your kids involved. I know it's tough to get rid of things, but think about how much someone else will really enjoy something you never wear.

For dinner, include some *Blissfully Frisky Foods* (on page 159).

Today I felt Bliss when: _____

_____

_____

Day 8

Today's Date: _____

Start off the day with a *Dandelion Bloat-Buster Tea* (recipe on page 95) instead of coffee.

Over the past week, have you been hard on yourself at all? For instance, have you looked in the mirror and silently (or even worse, out loud) called yourself fat, or have you made a mistake and not forgiven yourself for it? Write down two ways you've been hard on yourself.

_____

_____

The next time you try to insult yourself, write down two positive things you can tell yourself instead. Like: I'm a hot mama, or I'm a clever creature. You can be as silly, raunchy, or cheesy as you like as long as the end result is that you feel better about yourself and remember that you may be flawed like the rest of us, but you're still amazing.

_____

_____

Do 22 minutes of *Bliss-ercise* or regular exercise today. (Examples on page 90.)

*Pet owners: If your pet is due for a Pet Bliss treatment (found in Chapter 13, "Pet Bliss"), today is the day. Your pet won't mind the extra attention!

Perform a nails treatment (in Chapter 6, "Nails Bliss") that you need the most.

Today I felt Bliss when: _____

_____

_____

Day 9

Today's Date: _____

Make a batch of your favorite *DIY Blissful Energy Bars* (on page 136), and nosh on them about an hour before your energy typically begins to wane (based on the data you collected during the Living Bliss Plan).

When an energy slump is coming on, get up and stretch, do some jumping jacks, take a walk around the block, or if you have time, hit the gym. Spending some energy actually makes you feel more energetic.

Perform the *Incredible Shrinking Woman Wrap* (on page 94).

Either continue with your closet Bliss mission by focusing on a new section of it for 22 minutes, or spend those minutes decluttering, organizing, or beautifying a different area of your home, car, or office. Don't get discouraged if progress is slow; progress of any kind is wonderful!

Do 22 minutes of *Bliss-ercise* or regular exercise today. (Examples on page 90.)

Today I felt Bliss when: _____

_____

_____

Day 10

Today's Date: _____

Start off the day with a *Dandelion Bloat-Buster Tea* (recipe on page 95) instead of coffee.

Have a Bliss daydream today. Let your imagination run wild. Where does your mind drift to first? A romantic interlude on a beach? A big promotion at work? An exotic vacation? Write down a few thoughts here:

_____

_____

Now, think about one way, even if it's a small way, that you can work toward experiencing this daydream in real life or at least getting a little taste of it this month. Some ideas: Plan a candlelit evening at home with your partner, pitch an idea to your boss that could get you noticed, or place an exotic flower arrangement in your living room.

_____

_____

Do 22 minutes of *Bliss-ercise* or regular exercise. (Examples on page 90.)

Perform a skin treatment (in Chapter 3, "Skin Bliss") that applies the most to you.

*Moms: If you've been schlepping around the house in a sweat suit or pajamas too much lately, pick a cute outfit and a pair of heels today. Even if you're not going anywhere in particular, sometimes it's nice to feel sexy!

Spend 22 minutes decluttering, organizing, or beautifying a space that needs a little extra attention.

Today I felt Bliss when: _____

_____

_____

Day 11

Today's Date: _____

Either wake up eight minutes early today or stay up eight minutes later than usual and spend the time doing anything that gives you Bliss. I hope I don't have to say this, but this activity should not be paying bills, looking over your child's homework, or plucking your eyebrows. This should be a relaxing, indulgent activity like reading a gossip magazine or catching up on your reality TV shows.

Do 22 minutes of *Bliss-ercise* or regular exercise today. (Examples on page 90.)

Perform a hair treatment (in Chapter 5, "Hair Bliss") that applies the most to you.

Today I felt Bliss when: _____
_____
_____

Day 12

Today's Date: _____

Do 22 minutes of *Bliss-ercise* or regular exercise today. (Examples on page 90.)

How will you give Bliss away to someone else today? Get creative!

_____

_____

Perform a nails treatment (in Chapter 6, "Nails Bliss") that applies the most to you.

OK, ladies, I have an idea for you. Why not pick one or two of the Man Bliss treatments and do them with a girlfriend instead? A huge part of Bliss is bonding with your friends, and this could be a fun, silly way to do just that.

Today I felt Bliss when: _____

_____

_____

Day 13

Today's Date: _____

Start off the day with a *Dandelion Bloat-Buster Tea* (recipe on page 95) instead of coffee.

Do 22 minutes of *Bliss-ercise* or regular exercise. (Examples on page 90.)

Perform a body treatment (in Chapter 7, "Body Bliss") that applies the most to you.

Spend 22 minutes decluttering, organizing, or beautifying any particular space in your home that's taking your Bliss away.

*Moms: Get the kids involved to show them that it can be fun and to set an example for them that what you don't need anymore can benefit others.

Today I felt Bliss when: _____

_____

_____

Day 14

Today's Date: _____

No *Bliss-ercise* or exercise today—it's your rest day.

Ladies, you're halfway through the Bliss Plan! How are you feeling? Do five minutes of Bliss reflection. Write down your favorite treatments or a couple Blissful tidbits you've learned about yourself.

_____

_____

Perform the *Ooh-La-La Lavender Pore Cleanser* (recipe on page 33).

If possible, give yourself a break from makeup today. After washing your face, just put on moisturizer, sunscreen, and lip balm. If you have a big event that you want to glam up for, let your skin be cosmetics-free for as much of the day as you can.

For dinner, include some *Blissfully Frisky Foods* (on page 159). These will rev up your (and his) engine, but even if that's not your goal, they're great for your overall health. My favorites are ginger and bananas. How about a sweet fruit salad with banana, mango, pineapple, pears, and minced garlic? Hello, yummy!

Today I felt Bliss when: _____

_____

_____

Day 15

Today's Date: _____

Think about the last time you were envious of something or focused on a material object you wanted that was out of your league financially. Write down what it was.

_____

_____

Now, to put that material object into perspective, write something in your life that you're deeply grateful for (such as your family, your health, or your humor).

_____

_____

It's kind of astonishing how silly and small that material object suddenly seems when you look at the big picture, right?

Do 22 minutes of *Bliss-ercise* or regular exercise today. (Examples on page 90.)

*Pet owners: If your pet is due for a Pet Bliss treatment (found in Chapter 13, "Pet Bliss"), today's the day.

Have fun doing a Man Bliss treatment on your guy.

Today I felt Bliss when: _____

_____

_____

Day 16

Today's Date: _____

Start off the day with a *Dandelion Bloat-Buster Tea* (recipe on page 95) instead of coffee.

Do 22 minutes of *Bliss-ercise* or regular exercise today. (Examples on page 90.)

Make a batch of your favorite *DIY Blissful Energy Bars* (on page 136), and nosh on them about an hour before your energy typically begins to wane (based on the data you collected during the Living Bliss Plan).

Spend 22 minutes decluttering, organizing, or beautifying one of your environments.

Today I felt Bliss when: _____

_____

_____

Day 17

Today's Date: _____

Do 22 minutes of *Bliss-ercise* or regular exercise today. (Examples on page 90.)

Take a moment to reflect on the past couple of weeks and think about how you've reacted when someone or something has made an attempt at stealing your Bliss. How did you handle it? How would you handle it next time? Write it down. _____

_____

_____

Perform a face treatment (in Chapter 4, "Face Bliss") that applies the most to you.

Today I felt Bliss when: _____

_____

_____

Day 18

Today's Date: _____

Wake up seven to eight minutes early today, and spend the time doing anything that gives you Bliss. Remember, this activity should be relaxing and self-indulgent!

Do 22 minutes of *Bliss-ercise* or regular exercise today. (Examples on page 90.)

Perform a body treatment (in Chapter 7, "Body Bliss") that applies the most to you.

What type of energy will you give off to others today? Even if you're tired, frustrated, or overwhelmed, make a promise to yourself to smile and make the best of every situation. Laugher is a great equalizer, so find a way to share a good laugh with someone today.

Today I felt Bliss when: _____

_____

_____

Day 19

Today's Date: _____

Have you been listening harder to your inner voice? Spending no more time than 30 seconds, think about what your inner voice is telling you. Write it down.

_____

_____

What's one simple thing you can do today to get one step closer to whatever your inner voice is telling you to do?

_____

_____

Do 22 minutes of *Bliss-ercise* or regular exercise today. (Examples on page 90.)

Perform a skin treatment (in Chapter 3, "Skin Bliss") that applies the most to you.

Spend 22 minutes decluttering, organizing, or beautifying one of your environments.

Today I felt Bliss when: _____

_____

_____

Day 20

Today's Date: _____

Start off the day with a *Dandelion Bloat-Buster Tea* (recipe on page 95) instead of coffee.

Do 22 minutes of *Bliss-ercise* or regular exercise today. (Examples on page 90.)

*Moms: Make some time today for bonding with your kids while feeling entertained yourself. Refer to the *So Happy Together* list on page 167 for a few ideas. This can be just a few minutes or longer, depending on your schedule.

Perform a hair treatment (in Chapter 5, "Hair Bliss") that applies the most to you.

Today I felt Bliss when: _____

_____

_____

Day 21

Today's Date: _____

Three weeks are gone, girls! Look in the mirror this morning. Is your hair shiner? Is your skin glowing? Are your eyes brighter? Do you feel more rested? Take a few minutes to savor the progress you've made and to congratulate yourself, you gorgeous woman! If you've gotten off track, then today is the day to get back to it. You can do this!

No *Bliss-erise* or exercise today—it's your rest day.

Perform a nails treatment (in Chapter 6, "Nails Bliss") that applies the most to you.

For dinner, include some Blissfully Frisky Foods (on page 159). These will rev up your (and his) engine, but even if that's not your goal, they're great for your overall health.

Today I felt Bliss when: _____

_____

_____

Day 22

Today's Date: _____

Write on your bathroom mirror in red lipstick the following words: "You are magnificent." (Other adjectives to choose from: Blissful, stunning, hot, or gorgeous.) Keep it up there through the rest of this plan, and every time you pass by it, let it be a little reminder of how fabulous you truly are.

Do 22 minutes of *Bliss-ercise* or regular exercise today. (Examples on page 90.)

*Moms: Show your kids how fun this can be and include them in your workout routine (as long as you're able to do so safely!).

*Pet owners: If your pet is due for a Pet Bliss treatment (found in Chapter 13, "Pet Bliss"), go for it today! Your pet won't mind the extra attention!

Perform a body treatment (in Chapter 7, "Body Bliss") that applies the most to you.

Today I felt Bliss when: _____

_____

_____

Day 23

Today's Date: _____

Start off the day with a *Dandelion Bloat-Buster Tea* (recipe on page 95) instead of coffee.

Do 22 minutes of *Bliss-ercise* or regular exercise today. (Examples on page 90.)

Perform a skin treatment (in Chapter 3, "Skin Bliss") that applies the most to you.

Make a batch of your favorite *DIY Blissful Energy Bars* (on page 136), and nosh on them about an hour before your energy typically begins to wane (based on the data you collected during the Living Bliss Plan).

Spend 22 minutes decluttering, organizing, and beautifying one of your environments.

Today I felt Bliss when: _____

_____

_____

Day 24

Today's Date: _____

Write down your favorite childhood memory. It can be anything at all from summer swimming with friends to riding on your dad's shoulders while eating ice cream, or it could just be receiving a good grade from your favorite teacher.

_____

_____

Now, think about how you can recreate this feeling today. Maybe it's by finding a picture online that reminds you of it and hanging the photo on your fridge, or maybe it's calling a family member and reminiscing. Find a way to relive past Bliss so you can experience a modified version of it again in the present.

Do 22 minutes of *Bliss-ercise* or regular exercise today. (Examples on page 90.)

Perform a hair treatment (in Chapter 5, "Hair Bliss") that applies the most to you.

Today I felt Bliss when: _____

_____

_____

Day 25

Today's Date: _____

Commit to take an eight-minute Bliss timeout today. The world will not stop spinning on its axis if you simply put your to-do list aside for less than 10 minutes, I promise. Go for a walk, take a nap, or let your mind wander in any form or fashion. (Tip: Set an egg timer if you're worried about getting too carried away!)

Do 22 minutes of *Bliss-ercise* or regular exercise today. (Examples on page 90.)

Perform a nails treatment (in Chapter 6, "Nails Bliss") that applies the most to you.

Today I felt Bliss when: _____

_____

_____

Day 26

Today's Date: _____

How will you give Bliss away today? Get creative! _____

_____

_____

Have a *Dandelion Bloat-Buster Tea* (recipe on page 95) this afternoon with a light snack.

Do 22 minutes of *Bliss-ercise* or regular exercise today. (Examples on page 90.)

Perform a body treatment (in Chapter 7, "Body Bliss") that applies the most to you.

Today I felt Bliss when: _____

_____

_____

Day 27

Today's Date: _____

Do 22 minutes of *Bliss-ercise* or regular exercise today. (Examples on page 90.)

Perform a skin treatment (in Chapter 3, "Skin Bliss") that applies the most to you.

Spend 22 minutes enhancing the space in which you spend the most amount of time. Give it a few special touches...simple, inexpensive changes to the space that will make you smile when you're in it.

Today I felt Bliss when: _____

_____

_____

Day 28

Today's Date: _____

No *Bliss-ercise* or exercise today—it's your rest day.

Perform a hair treatment (in Chapter 5, "Hair Bliss") that applies the most to you.

How will you give Bliss away today? Get creative! _____

_____

_____

Take a little extra "you" time today and style your hair, apply some pretty makeup, and put on your favorite earrings. Then look in the mirror for at least 30 seconds, smile at yourself, and truly appreciate what a beautiful person you are, inside and out.

Today I felt Bliss when: _____

_____

_____

Day 29

Today's Date: _____

Start off the day with a *Dandelion Bloat-Buster Tea* (recipe on page 95) instead of coffee.

Do 22 minutes of *Bliss-ercise* or regular exercise today. (Examples on page 90.)

*Pet owners: If your pet is due for a Pet Bliss treatment (found in Chapter 13, "Pet Bliss"), go for it today! Your pet won't mind the extra attention!

Perform a nails treatment (in Chapter 6, "Nails Bliss") that applies the most to you.

How will you give Bliss away today? Get creative! _____

_____

_____

Today I felt Bliss when: _____

_____

_____

Day 30

Today's Date: _____

Do 22 minutes of *Bliss-ercise* or regular exercise today. (Examples on page 90.)

Have fun doing a Man Bliss treatment of your (and, OK, his) choice on your guy.

*Moms: Make some time today for bonding with your kids while feeling entertained yourself. Refer to the *So Happy Together* list on page 167 for a few ideas. This can be just a few minutes or longer, depending on your schedule.

Spend 22 minutes decluttering, organizing, or beautifying an area in your home, car or office.

For dinner, include some *Blissfully Frisky Foods* (on page 159). These will rev up your (and his) engine, but even if that's not your goal, they're great for your overall health.

Today I felt Bliss when: _____

_____

_____

Now, it's time for the moment of truth! Go back to Chapter 1 and retake the Bliss Quiz. Record your new, improved current Bliss Factor.

What is your new Bliss Factor? _____

If you truly followed this plan for 30 days (only you know if you "cheated!"), there's no question in my mind that you have boosted your Bliss factor big time. Can you believe how much progress you made in just 30 days? I'm not saying it was easy, but the fact of the matter is that 30 days have passed and you've added Bliss not only to your life but also to your partner's, pet's, strangers', and I hope everyone with whom you've been in contact. That's how Bliss works—it spreads like wildfire! You can always refer to this plan for inspiration or just do the whole thing all over again anytime. You've ingrained some fabulous new habits that I hope you'll continue.

I learned a lot about myself and my own Bliss while writing this book and creating these plans. I really believe if you become more aware of the Bliss in your life, more Bliss will naturally come to you. Congratulations on bringing more happiness to your life this month. This book has made me so much more aware of the joys in my own life, and it brought to light certain Bliss stealers and boosters. It's an emotional process sometimes, and I think that's important. Don't be afraid to do a little soul searching and get to know yourself on a deeper level. Yes, it can be frightening, but it's so rewarding in the end.

· · ·

Before I go, I'd like to share one last, very significant story from my life. I was just 12 years old when I discovered something that I knew would change my life: television reporting. I was watching TV in our living room while my mom was making dinner. Jessica Savitch was reporting the news (I'm talking 1977), and I was mesmerized. She was strong, authoritative, attractive, and I thought she even looked a little like an older version of me. I turned to my mother as she was stirring a pot of stew. Pointing at the television, I blurted out, "Mom! I want to do that when I grow up!" She stopped her stirring, lifted her head, and firmly declared, "Well, then you will," and went right back to her stew. In an instant, she had just validated my goal, and I never once questioned it even though it made absolutely no sense. I mean, we had zero connections in the worlds of journalism, TV, or Hollywood. We were a small family living in a suburb of Detroit—Detroit for Pete's sake. My father was a Scottish immigrant who worked as a carpenter, and we certainly didn't have enough money to send me chasing after some pipe dream. So, where did I get the idea that I could ever have career in television? From inside my heart and my mother's affirmation, that's where!

I have been very fortunate to be able to do what I do and to have found success in my chosen career. There have been a lot of twists and turns, but it's all helped me develop a passion to help women, all women, see that Bliss isn't a privilege to be experienced only by the elite. We all deserve happiness. That's why I wrote this book. I want you to find Bliss in the least expected places, in the craziest of ways, and on an everyday basis. I know I'm lucky to have the kind of family who never told me I couldn't live out my dreams. It didn't even occur to me that pursuing my passion was a long shot. I realize you may not have someone in your life to validate your hopes and desires—or perhaps you've been told you're out of your mind to dream big or dream at all. I hope after reading this book you now know that you don't actually need that validation from someone else. You can give up the tired, old excuses, ignore your inner (or outer!) frenemy, and stack the deck in your favor in hundreds of little ways to get to your Bliss, regardless of what anyone else has to say about it.

Repeat after me: "I want to experience Bliss every day of my life, no matter what happens." If you really mean that, then I can tell you: "Well, then you will!"

In Bliss,

Kym Douglas

Resources

Chapter 2

"bliss." 2005. *The Merriam-Webster Dictionary*. Merriam Webster: Springfield, MA.

Part 2 Introduction

Ansel, K. 2012. Shrink Your Belly with Food. *Prevention Magazine*. http://www.prevention.com/weight-loss/diets/shrink-your-belly-food/3-add--potassium-rich-foods#ixzz1wOyPn1rv

Chang, L. 2011. Top 10 Foods for Healthy Hair. WebMD. http://www.webmd.com/healthy-beauty/features/top-10-foods-for-healthy-hair

Duse, E. Coconut Oil. TLC Family. http://tlc.howstuffworks.com/family/coconut-oil1.htm/printable

Ehrlich, S. 2011. Omega-3 Fatty Acids. University of Maryland Medical Center. http://www.umm.edu/altmed/articles/omega-3-000316.htm

Eisenstein, D. 2005. 6 Superfoods for Healthy Hair. *Ladies Home Journal*. http://www.lhj.com/style/hair/hair-care/6-superfoods-for-healthy-hair/

George Mateljan Foundation. Manganese. http://whfoods.org/genpage.php?pfriendly=1&tname=nutrient&dbid=77

Haas, E. 2011. Role of Potassium in Maintaining Health. *Periodic Paralysis International*. http://hkpp.org/patients/potassium-health

Higdon, J. 2004. Potassium. Linus Pauling Institute: Micronutrient Research for Optimum Health. Oregon State University. http://lpi.oregonstate.edu/infocenter/minerals/potassium/

Kadey, M. Boost energy, strengthen immune system and more. *Women's Health*. http://www.womenshealthmag.com/nutrition/super-foods-for-a-healthier-you?cat=11450&tip=11469

National Agriculture Library. Nutrition data for coconut milk. USDA. http://ndb.nal.usda.gov/ndb/foods/show/3725

National Agriculture Library. Nutrition data for coconut oil. USDA. http://ndb.nal.usda.gov/ndb/foods/show/607

National Agriculture Library. Nutrition data for coconut water. USDA. http://ndb.nal.usda.gov/ndb/foods/show/3727

Nelson, J; and Zeratsky, K. 2012. Nutrition and healthy eating. What's the buzz behind coconut water? Mayo Clinic.

Nevin, KG; and Rajamohan, T. 2004. Beneficial effects of virgin coconut oil on lipid parameters and in vitro LDL oxidation. *Clinical Biochemistry*; 37(9):830-5.

Rele, AS; and Mohile, RB. 2003. Effect of mineral oil, sunflower oil, and coconut oil on prevention of hair damage. *Journal of Cosmetic Science*; 54(2):175-92

Risher, B. The Best Foods for Healthy Hair. *Men's Health*. http://www.menshealth.com/spotlight/hair/best-food-for-healthy-hair.php

Ruetsch, SB; Kamath, YK; Rele, AS; and Mohile RB. 2011. Secondary Ion mass spectrometric investigation of penetration of coconut and mineral oils into human hair fibers: relevance to hair damage. *Journal of Cosmetic Science*; 52(3): 169-84.

Saat, M; Singh, R; Sirisinghe, RG; and Nawawi, M. 2002. Rehydration after exercise with fresh young coconut water, carbohydrate-electrolyte beverage and plain water. *Journal of Physiological Anthropology and Applied Human Science*; 21(2):93-104.

Saling, J. 2011. Eat Right for Your Hair Type. WebMD. http://www.webmd.com/healthy-beauty/hair-health-11/eat-hair-type?page=1

Temme, EH; Mensink, RP; and Hornstra, G. 1996. Comparison of the effects of diets rich in lauric, palmitic, or oleic acids on serum lipids and lipoproteins in healthy women and men. *The American Journal of Clinical Nutrition*; 63(6): 897-903.

Trost, L.B.; et al. 2006. The diagnosis and treatment of iron deficiency and its potential relationship to hair loss. *Journal of the American Academy of Dermatology*; 54(5):824-44.

Uscher, J. 2012. Nutrients for healthy skin. WebMD. http://www.webmd.com/healthy-beauty/features/skin-nutrition

Williams, C. 2008. 8 steps to healthy skin, hair and nails. Healthy Food Guide. http://www.healthyfood.co.nz/comment/97

Zelman, K. 2010. The Truth About Coconut Water. WebMD. http://www
.webmd.com/food-recipes/features/truth-about-coconut-water

Zeratsky, K. 2010. Weight Loss, Can Coconut Oil Help Me Lose Weight?
Mayo Clinic.

Zerello, A. 2010. 8 Foods to eat for beautiful skin. Shine from Yahoo. http://
shine.yahoo.com/great-skin/8-foods-to-eat-for-beautiful-skin-1186141.html

Chapter 3

Acne.org. Adult Acne. http://www.acne.org/adult-acne.html

Al-Waili, NS. 2005. Mixture of honey, beeswax, and olive oil inhibits growth
of Staphylococcus aureus and Candido albicans. *Archives of Medical
Research*; 36(1):10-3.

Al-Waili, NS. 2004. An alternative treatment for pityriasis versicolor, tinea
cruris, tinea corporis and tinea faciei with topical application of honey,
olive oil and beeswax mixture: an open pilot study. *Complementary
Therapies in Medicine*; 12(1):45-7.

American Academy of Dermatology. 2009. Dermatologists shed light on
common pigmentation problems and solutions in skin of color. http://
www.aad.org/stories-and-news/news-releases/dermatologists-shed-light-
on-common-pigmentation-problems-and-solutions-in-skin-of-color

American Cancer Society. 2008. Lipoic Acid. http://www.
cancer.org/Treatment/TreatmentsandSideEffects/
ComplementaryandAlternativeMedicine/
PharmacologicalandBiologicalTreatment/lipoic-acid

Beitner, H. 2003. Randomized, placebo-controlled, double blind study on
the clinical efficacy of a cream containing 5% alpha-lipoic acid related
to photo ageing of facial skin. *The British Journal of Dermatology*;
149(4):841-9.

Berson, D. 2009. Acne Fact Sheet. U.S. Department of Health and
Human Services Office on Women's Health. http://womenshealth.gov/
publications/our-publications/fact-sheet/acne.cfm#h

Boddie, A; et al. 2010. Supplement with encapsulated vegetable and fruit
juice powder concentrate improves microcirculation and ultrastructure
in human skin. *The Journal of the Federation of American Societies for
Experimental Biology*; Ib338.

Bradley, M. A complete guide on moisturizers. HealthGuidance. http://
www.healthguidance.org/entry/14333/1/A-Complete-Guide-on-
Moisturizer.html

Brown, NJ; et al. 1994. The effect of cryotherapy on the cremaster muscle microcirculation in vivo. *British Journal of Cancer*; 69(4):706-710.

Caporimo, A. 2011. 7 bad skin mistakes that add years. MSNBC. http://today.msnbc.msn.com/id/42342986/ns/today-style/t/bad-skin-mistakes-can-add-years/

CBS News. 2010. Bag Balm Becomes Popular Problem Salver. http://www.cbsnews.com/stories/2010/02/01/health/main6162364.shtml

Cleveland Clinic. 2011. Understanding the ingredients in skin care products. http://my.clevelandclinic.org/healthy_living/skin_care/hic_understanding_the_ingredients_in_skin_care_products.aspx

Cousin, PJ. 2001. Anti-wrinkle treatments for perfect skin. Massachusetts: Storey books.

Collins, K. 2006. Olive oil a rich source of antioxidants. MSNBC. http://www.msnbc.msn.com/id/11758647/ns/health-fitness/t/olive-oil-brings-more-flavor-your-diet/

Colino, S. What are those ingredients in your skin-care products? Real Simple. http://www.realsimple.com/beauty-fashion/skincare/what-ingredients-skin-care-products-10000001684994/index.html

Dweck, A. 1995. Natural solutions to cellulite. Soap Perfumery and Cosmetics; 68(10):45-9.

Fisher, GJ; et al. 2008. Looking older: fibroblast collapse and therapeutic implications. Archives of Dermatology; 44(5).

Gilchrest, BA. 1996. A review of skin ageing and its medical therapy. The British Journal of Dermatology; 135(6):867-75.

Grimes, PE. 1999. The safety and efficiency of salicylic acid chemical peels in darker racial-ethnic groups. Dermatologic Surgery; 25(1):18-22.

Hang, YD; et al. 1987. Microbial production of citric acid by solid state fermentation of kiwifruit peel. Journal of Food Science; 52(1):226-227.

Hercberg S; et al. 2004. The SU.VI.MAX Study: a randomized, placebo-controlled trial of the health effects of antioxidant vitamins and minerals. Archives of Internal Medicine; 164(21): 2335-42.

Huh, CH; et al. 2003. A randomized, double-blind, placebo-controlled trial of vitamin C iontophoresis in melasma. Dermatology; 206(4):316-20.

Kirchheimer, S. 1995. The Doctor's Book of Home Remedies II. Boston: Bantam.

MacKay, D; and Miller, A. 2003. Nutritional support for wound healing. Alternative Medicine Review; 8.4.

Mayo Clinic. 2010. Wrinkle creams: your guide to younger looking skin. http://www.mayoclinic.com/health/wrinklecreams/SN00010/ NSECTIONGROUP=2

Mayo Clinic. 2010. Moisturizers: options for softer skin. http://www.mayoclinic.com/health/moisturizers/SN00042

McCullough, JL; and Kelly, KM. 2006. Prevention and treatment of skin aging. Annals of the New York Academy of Sciences; 1067:323-31.

Mindell, E. 2002. Amazing Apple Cider Vinegar. New York: Contemporary Books.

National Institutes of Health. 2010. Salicylic acid topical. http://www.nlm.nih.gov/medlineplus/druginfo/meds/a607072.html

Oliver, JF; and Aff, R. 1996. Rubiginosa effects on skin burns. Fats & Oils Journal; No.25.

Oregon State University. 2007. Micronutrient information center: Vitamin A. http://lpi.oregonstate.edu/infocenter/vitamins/vitaminA/

Pellis, L; et al. 2008. High folic acid increases cell turnover and lowers differentiation and iron content in human HT29 colon cancer cells. The British Journal of Nutrition; 99(4):703-8.

Penniston, K. Citric acid and kidney stones. UW Hospital and Clinics. http://www.uwhealth.org/files/uwhealth/docs/pdf/kidney_citric_acid.pdf

Rattan, SI; and Sodagam, L. 2005. Gerontomodulatory and youth-preserving effects of zeatin on human skin fibroblasts undergoing aging in vitro. Rejuvenation Research; 8(1):46-57.

Rawlings, AV. 2006. Cellulite and its treatment. International Journal of Cosmetic Science; 24(3):175-190.

Ross, B. Acne 101. 2009. The University of Texas Health Science Center at Houston. HealthLeader. http://publicaffairs.uth.tmc.edu/hleader/archive/Dermatology/2009/acne101-0304.htm

Schwarcz, J. 2000. Shania Twain's Secret to Soft and Supple Skin. CBS News.

Siddons, S. Lactic acid skin care. Discovery Fit and Health. http://health.howstuffworks.com/skin-care/beauty/lactic-acid-skin-care1.htm

Stewart, K. 2009. The skin care benefits of alpha hydroxy acids. Everyday Health. http://www.everydayhealth.com/skin-and-beauty/alpha-hydroxy-acids.aspx

Stiller, MJ; et al. 1996. Topical 8% glycolic acid and 8% L-lactic acid creams for the treatment of photodamaged skin. A double-blind vehicle-controlled clinical trial. Archives of Dermatology; 132(6):631-6.

Surjushe, A; et al. 2008. Aloe vera: a short review. Indian Journal of Dermatology; 53(4):163-6.

Top10King. 2011. Top 10 weirdest facial treatments for wrinkles. http://top10king.com/top-10-weirdest-facial-treatments-for-wrinkles/

Tse, TW. 2010. Hydroquinone for skin lightening: safety profile, duration of use and when should we stop? The Journal of Dermatological Treatment; 21(5):272-5.

University of Maryland Medical Center. 2011. Brewer's Yeast. http://www.umm.edu/altmed/articles/brewers-yeast-000288.htm

USDA. 2012. National nutrient database for standard reference. http://ndb.nal.usda.gov/ndb/foods/show/2956

U.S. Food and Drug Administration. 2011. Alpha hydroxy acids in cosmetics. http://www.fda.gov/cosmetics/productandingredientsafety/selectedcosmeticingredients/ucm107940.htm

van Leeuwen, R; et al. 2005. Dietary intake of antioxidants and risk of age-related macular degeneration. Journal of the American Medical Association; 294(24):3101-7.

WebMD. Choosing your skin care products: know your ingredients. http://www.webmd.com/healthy-beauty/cosmetic-procedures-products-2?page=2

WebMD. 2011. Skin lightening products. http://www.webmd.com/healthy-beauty/skin-lightening-products?page=2

WebMD. Wrinkle fillers. http://www.webmd.com/healthy-beauty/cosmetic-procedures-collagen

Yosipovitch, G; and Hu, J. 2003. The importance of skin pH. HMP Communications, LLC; 11(3):88-93.

Zander, E; and Weisman, S. 1992. Treatment of Acne Vulgaris with Salicylic Acid Pads. Clinical Therapeutics; 14(2):247-53.

Chapter 4

American Society of Plastic Surgeons. 2011. Plastic Surgery Statistics Report. http://www.plasticsurgery.org/Documents/news-resources/statistics/2011-statistics/2011-cosmetic-procedures-trends-statistics.pdf

American Academy of Cosmetic Dentistry. 2007. Cosmetic dentistry state of the industry. http://www.aacd.com/proxy.php?filename=files/Footer%20Nav/Media%20Room/Surveys/AACD%20State%20of%20the%20Cosmetic%20Dentistry%20Industry%202011.pdf

Baumann, L; Woolery-Lloyd, H; Friedman, A. 2009. Natural" ingredients in cosmetic dermatology. Journal of Drugs in Dermatology; 8(6 Suppl): s5-9.

Bogdanov, S. 2009. The Beeswax Book: Uses and Trade. Bee Product Science. http://bee-hexagon.net/files/file/fileE/Wax/WaxBook1.pdf

Consumer Reports. 2010. Do eye creams make a visible difference? http://www.consumerreports.org/health/healthy-living/beauty-personal-care/wrinkle-products/eye-creams/index.htm.

Dawes, C. 1984 Stimulus effects on protein and electrolyte concentrations in parotid saliva. The Journal of Physiology; 346:579-88.

DiFrisco, M. 2007. Cosmetic dentistry continues to surge. American Academy of Cosmetic Dentistry. http://www.aacd.com/index.php?module=cms&page=723

Firoz, EF; et al. 2009. Lip plumper contact urticaria. Journal of the American Academy of Dermatology; 60(5):861-3.

Fleming, O. 2012. Egg white facelift and cinnamon lip-plumper: Lisa Rinna reveals the kitchen essentials that keep her looking young, and the science that proves they work. Daily Mail. http://www.dailymail.co.uk/femail/article-2145400/Lisa-Rinna-reveals-kitchen-essentials-looking-young.html

Goldfaden, G. 2009. Revitalize aging skin with topical vitamin C. Life Extension Magazine. http://www.lef.org/magazine/mag2009/may2009_Revitalizing-Aging-Skin-with-Topical-Vitamin-C_01.htm

Higdon, J. 2006. Vitamin C. Linus Pauling Institute: Micronutrient Research for Optimum Health. http://lpi.oregonstate.edu/infocenter/vitamins/vitaminC/

Levitt, S. 2011. Lip plumpers: do they work? WebMD. http://www.webmd.com/healthy-beauty/features/bigger-lips-lip-plumping-products

Lieberman, J. 2006. Do teeth whiteners really work? MSNBC. http://today.msnbc.msn.com/id/15520798/ns/today-money/t/will-whiteners-give-you-movie-star-smile/#.T9knzlI1WiA

Mapes, D. 2007. Blindingly white: teeth bleaching gone too far. MSNBC. http://www.msnbc.msn.com/id/15309784/#.T9kohlI1WiA

The Renfrew Center Foundation. 2012. New survey results indicate there's more to make-up use than meets the eye. http://renfrewcenter.com/sites/default/files/press_release_pdfs/Barefaced and Beautiful Release - FINAL.pdf

Timmel, K. 2008. How to whiten your teeth naturally. Health Magazine. http://www.health.com/health/article/0,,20410846,00.html

Rele, AS; Mohile, RB. 2003. Effect of mineral oil, sunflower oil, and coconut oil on prevention of hair damage. Journal of Cosmetic Science; 54(2):175-192.

Vidt, DG; and Bergfeld, WF. 1997. Cosmetic use of alpha-hydroxy acids. Cleveland Clinic Journal of Medicine; 64(6): 327-9.

Chapter 5

Amor, KT; Rashid, RM; and Mirmirani, P. 2010. Does D matter? The role of vitamin D in hair disorders and hair follicle cycling. Dermatology Online Journal; 16(2):3

Argan Oil Society. 2010. Argan Oil for hairs—an incredible natural gift. http://www.arganoilsociety.org/argan-oil-benefits-for-hair/

Consumer Reports. 2010. ShopSmart Hair Poll Gets to the Roots: 60% Like It or Love It, 4% Hate It. http://pressroom.consumerreports.org/pressroom/2010/04/shopsmart-hair-poll-gets-to-the-roots-60-like-it-or-love-it-4-hate-it.html

Covello, L. 2012. $950 for a haircut and rising. FOXBusiness http://www.foxbusiness.com/personal-finance/2012/05/31/50-for-haircut-and-rising/

Goins, L. 2011. Shampoo, Shampoo everywhere—but which one's right for your hair? WebMD. http://www.webmd.com/healthy-beauty/features/shampoo-shampoo-everywhere-but-which-ones-right-for-your-hair

Halvorson, C. Uses for baking soda: health and beauty. Discovery Fit & Health. http://health.howstuffworks.com/wellness/hygiene-tips/uses-for-baking-soda-health-and-beauty-ga.htm

Hatfield, H. 2011. 8 ways you're damaging your hair. WebMD. http://www.webmd.com/healthy-beauty/features/8-ways-youre-damaging-your-hair

Hellmich, N. 2010. Bad Hair day can hit women's self-esteem, wallet. USA TODAY. http://www.usatoday.com/news/health/2010-04-12-bad-hair_N.htm

Hillenmeyer, J. 2012. 2011 salon industry study shows growth. Modern Salon. http://www.modernsalon.com/news/beauty-news/-New-2011-Professional-Salon-Industry-Haircare-Study-Shows-Strong-139012939.html

Holmes, E. 2011. The Blow-Dry Bar Scene. The Wall Street Journal. http://online.wsj.com/article/SB10001424052970204831304576595322366093848.html

Hygiene Council. Mold in the home: Fact Sheet. http://www.hygienecouncil.org/Portals/1/pdf/Media_Mould_in_the_Home_Fact_Sheet.pdf

Kozolchyk, A. 2010. Gorgeous Hair at Any Age. WebMD. http://www .webmd.com/healthy-beauty/features/gorgeous-hair-at-any-age

Kwakman, PH; et al. 2010. How honey kills bacteria. Federation of American Societies for Experimental Biology; (7):2576-82.

Lansky, V. 2003. Baking Soda: Over 500 Fabulous, Fun and Frugal Uses You've Probably Never Thought Of, second edition. Minneapolis, MN: The Book Peddlers.

Larocca, A. 2007. Liquid Gold in Morocco. The New York Times. http:// travel.nytimes.com/2007/11/18/travel/tmagazine/14get-sourcing-caps. html

Matthews, M. Amazing Facts About Hair. Woman's Day. http://www. womansday.com/style-beauty/10-amazing-facts-about-hair-92040

Mayo Clinic. 2012. Hair Loss: Causers. http://www.mayoclinic.com/health/ hairloss/DS00278/DSECTION=causes

Meers, C. 2011. Trend Alert: Blowdry Bars. Marie Claire. http://www .marieclaire.com/hair-beauty/trends/blow-dry-bar-hair-trend

Mohile, RB; Rele RS. 2003. Effect of mineral oil, sunflower oil, and coconut oil on prevention of hair damage. Journal of Cosmetic Science; 54(2):175-92.

Parker, H. Top 10 foods for healthy hair. WebMD. http://www.webmd.com/ healthy-beauty/features/top-10-foods-for-healthy-hair

Polansky, MM; Murphy, EW. 1966. Vitamin B 6 components in fruits and nuts. Journal of American Dietetic Association; 48:109-111.

Sally Beauty Supply LLC. Argan oil: beauty magic for hair. http:// www.sallybeauty.com/argan-oil/BEAUTYSOLUTIONS_HAIR_ ARGAN,default,pg.html

Shapouri, B. Do you love your hair? The newest Dove survey found only 7 percent of women do. Glamour. http://www.glamour.com/beauty/blogs/ girls-in-the-beauty-department/2011/10/do-you-love-your-hair-the-newe. html

Swisher, HE. 1988. Avocado oil: from food use to skin care. Journal of American. Oil Chemists' Society; 65:1704-1706.

The Original Mane 'n Tail. Original Mane 'n Tail Shampoo. http://manentail. com/products/the-original-mane-n-tail-shampoo/

University of Maryland Medical Center. Amino acids: overview. Medical Encyclopedia. http://www.umm.edu/ency/article/002222.htm

University of Maryland Medical Center. Vitamin H (Biotin). http://www .umm.edu/altmed/articles/vitamin-h-000342.htm

WebMD. Find a vitamin or supplement: coconut oil. 2012. http://www
.webmd.com/vitamins-supplements/ingredientmono-1092-COCONUT%
20OIL.aspx?activeIngredientId=1092&activeIngredientName=
COCONUT%20OIL

Wilson, J. After winter's wrath, fix frizzy hair, dry lips and skin. CNN. http://
www.cnn.com/2011/HEALTH/02/17/winter.beauty.tips/index.html

Chapter 6

Alam, M; et al. 2011. Comparative stain removal properties of four
commercially available denture cleaning products: an in vitro study.
International Journal of Dental Hygiene; 9(1):37-42.

Berman, K. 2011. Nail abnormalities. National Institutes of Health. http://
www.nlm.nih.gov/medlineplus/ency/article/003247.htm

Chaturvedi, M. 2011. World's most expensive manicure to get you
glittering for $51,000. Born Rich. http://www.bornrich.com/entry/
get-glittering-with-worlds-most-expensive-manicure-worth-51000/

Douglas, J. 2011. Nail Polish: A big beauty trend of 2011. Shine from Yahoo.
http://shine.yahoo.com/beauty/nail-polish-is-the-biggest-beauty-
trend-of-2011.html

Edrogan, F; et al. 2011. Efficacy of Topical Anesthetics in the Treatment of
Ingrown Nail. Turkderm; 45(2):88-92.

Ehrlich, S. 2011. Bromelain. University of Maryland Medical Center. http://
www.umm.edu/altmed/articles/bromelain-000289.htm

Ferreira, J. 2010. DIY: 4 simple steps to strengthening your nails (with
garlic!). SELF.

http://www.self.com/beauty/blogs/beyondthebeautypages/2010/10/diy-
nail-treatment-strengthen.html

Good Housekeeping. Spa-like pedicures at home.

http://www.goodhousekeeping.com/beauty/nail-care/feet-first-aug03

Higdon, J. 2008. Biotin. Linus Pauling Institute: Micronutrient Research for
Optimum Health. http://lpi.oregonstate.edu/infocenter/vitamins/biotin/

Kwakman, PH; et al. 2010. How honey kills bacteria. Federation of American
Societies for Experimental Biology; (7):2576-82.

Langan, M. 2010. Aging changes in hair and nails. National Institutes of
Health. http://www.nlm.nih.gov/medlineplus/ency/article/004005.htm

Ludwig, J. 2012. Proven home remedies for common conditions. AARP.
http://www.aarp.org/health/conditions-treatments/info-08-2011/
home-remedies.3.html

Marie Claire. How to whiten yellow nails. http://www.marieclaire.com/
hair-beauty/how-to/nails-whiten-yellow

Martin, L. 2011. What your nails say about your health. WebMD. http://
www.webmd.com/healthy-beauty/ss/slideshow-nails-and-health

Mayo Clinic. 2011. Fingernails: do's and don'ts for healthy nails. Adult
Health. http://www.mayoclinic.com/health/nails/WO00020

Mayo Clinic. Lifestyle and home remedies: nail fungus. http://
www.mayoclinic.com/health/nail-fungus/DS00084/
DSECTION=lifestyle-and-home-remedies

National Cancer Institute. 2008. Garlic and cancer prevention. National
Cancer Institute Fact Sheet.

National Institutes of Health. 2011. Tea tree oil. http://www.nlm.nih.gov/
medlineplus/druginfo/natural/113.html

Prevention. 2011. 19 Bizarre home cures that work. http://www.prevention.
com/health/natural-remedies/19-bizarre-home-cures-work/
home-cure-vegetable-oil

Rondon, LJ; et al. 2010. Magneisum attenuates chronic hypersensitivity and
spinal cord NMDA receptor phosphorylation in a rat model of diabetic
neuropathic pain. The Journal of Physiology; 588(Pt 21):4205-15.

Siegel, R. 2011. Nail Polish Craze: America loves manicures! Lucky
Magazine. http://www.luckymag.com/blogs/luckyrightnow/2011/08/
nail-polish-craze-america-loves-manicures

Chapter 7

Abramson, E. 2011. Does my butt look big? Psychology Today. http://
www.psychologytoday.com/blog/its-not-just-baby-fat/201101/
does-make-my-butt-look-big

American Society of Plastic Surgeons. 2011. Statistics Report. http://
www.plasticsurgery.org/Documents/news-resources/statistics/2011-
statistics/2011_Stats_Full_Report.pdf%3E

Aschan, S. 2008. Solutions for post-workout pain. ABC News. http://
abcnews.go.com/Health/PainManagement/story?id=4115309&page=1

Baldauf, S; Palmer, K. 2012. 3 Healthy Habits that Aren't Worth the Cost. US
News and World Report. http://money.usnews.com/money/personal-
finance/articles/2012/03/13/3-healthy-habits-that-arent-worth-the-cost

Bilbey, DL; and Prabhakaran, VM. 1996. Muscle cramps and magnesium
deficiency: a case reports. Canadian Family Physician; 42:1348-51.

Boschmann M; et al. 2003. Water-induced thermogenesis. The Journal of Clinical Endocrinology and Metabolism; 88(12):6015-9.

Brett, J. Benefits of Vitamin A. Discovery fit & health. http://health. howstuffworks.com/wellness/food-nutrition/vitamin-supplements/ benefits-of-vitamin-a.htm

Cassimatis, G. 2008. Getting red carpet ready. MSN Diet & Nutrition. http://health.ninemsn.com.au/dietandnutrition/celebritytrends/695562/ getting-red-carpet-ready

CBS News. 2009. Body wraps: Way to look, feel slimmer?. http://www. cbsnews.com/2100-502343_162-3504860.html

Chitale, R. 2008. You feel what you eat. ABC News. http://abcnews.go.com/ Health/Depression/feel-eat/story?id=4387456#.T-NT9VI1WiA

Davis, R. 2007. A to Z of healthy holiday habits. Marie Claire. http://www .marieclaire.com/health-fitness/news/holiday-weight-loss-4

Decarbo, B. 2012. Quick cures/quack cures: is Epsom salt worth its salt? The Wall Street Journal. http://online.wsj.com/article/SB1000142405270230 3302504577327722133289222.html

Doheny, K. 2011. Body wraps: what to expect. WebMD.

http://www.webmd.com/healthy-beauty/features/ body-wraps-what-to-expect?page=2

Doheny, K. 2012.Choose dark chocolate for health benefits. WebMD. http://www.webmd.com/diet/news/20120424/ pick-dark-chocolate-health-benefits

Dole Diet Center. 2010. Eau de grapefruit. http://www.dole.com/ NutritionInstituteLanding/NI_Articles/NI_DoleDiet/NI_DoleDiet_Detail/ tabid/1058/Default.aspx?contentid=6185

Edwards, M. 2011. Healthy sugar alternatives. Organic Lifestyle Magazine. http://www.organiclifestylemagazine.com/healthy-sugar-alternatives/

Ehrlich, S. Peppermint. 2011. University of Maryland Medical Center. http:// www.umm.edu/altmed/articles/peppermint-000269.htm

Epsom Salt Council. Benefits of bathing with Epsom salt. http://www. epsomsaltcouncil.org/health/

Evert, A. 2011. Magnesium in diet. National Institutes of Health. http:// www.nlm.nih.gov/medlineplus/ency/article/002423.htm

Fitness Magazine. Our top 10 abs exercises. http://www.fitnessmagazine .com/workout/abs/exercises/top-10-abs-exercises/?page=8

Ghayur, MN; and Gilani, AH. 2005. Pharmacological basis for the medicinal use of ginger in gastrointestinal disorders. Digestive Diseases and Sciences; 50(10):1889-97.

Glamour. Sneaky ways to add exercise to your day (...and burn hundreds more calories!) http://www.glamour.com/health-fitness/2009/09/sneaky-ways-to-add-exercise-to-your-day#slide=1

Hartman, B. 6 habits to chisel a solid 6-pack. Men's Health. http://www.menshealth.com/mhlists/ab_strategies/Wake_Up_to_Water.php

Kadey, M. The best foods to boost your mood. SHAPE. http://www.shape.com/healthy-eating/diet-tips/best-foods-boost-your-mood

Knight, M. 2011. 9 Health benefits of dance. Everyday Health. http://www.everydayhealth.com/fitness-pictures/health-benefits-of-dance.aspx#/slide-1

Lagree, S. Home workout: grab a broomstick and give fat the brush-off. SELF. http://www.self.com/fitness/workouts/2007/09/fat-burning-slideshow#slide=3

Lawson, W. 2003. Omega-3s for boosting mood. Psychology Today. http://www.psychologytoday.com/articles/200301/omega-3s-boosting-mood

Levesque, W. 2005. Grapefruit scent has romantic effect, study finds. Tampa Bay Times. http://www.sptimes.com/2005/06/27/Business/Grapefruit_scent_has_.shtml

Levine, H; et al. 2007. Diet tricks of the stars. CNN Living. http://articles.cnn.com/2007-11-15/living/star.foods_1_big-bag-veggies-junk-food?_s=PM:LIVING

Levine, JA; et al. 2009. Move a Little, Lose a Lot. New York: Crown Publishing Group. 53.

Masters, M. 2010. Why your desk job is slowly killing you. MSNBC. http://www.msnbc.msn.com/id/39523298/ns/health-mens_health/t/why-your-desk-job-slowly-killing-you/

Men's Health. Happy foods. http://www.menshealth.co.uk/food-nutrition/superfoods/happy-foods-278392

Mayo Clinic. 2010. Walking: trim your waistline, improve your health. http://www.mayoclinic.com/health/walking/HQ01612

Mayo Clinic. 2011. Workplace exercises: how to burn calories at work. http://www.mayoclinic.com/health/office-exercise/SM00115

McCrady, SK; and Levine, JA. 2009. Sedentariness at work: how much do we really sit? Obesity; 17(11):2103-5.

Men's Health. The car-wash workout. http://www.menshealth.co.uk/building-muscle/bodyweight-exercises/the-car-wash-workout-423374

Morton, DP; Callister, R. 2010. Influence of posture and body type on the experience of exercise-related transient abdominal pain. Journal of Science and Medicine in Sport; 13(5):485-8.

National Institutes of Health. Office of Dietary Supplements Dietary Supplement Fact Sheet. Magnesium.

National Institutes of Health. 2011. Vitamin C. http://www.nlm.nih.gov/medlineplus/ency/article/002404.htm

National Institutes of Health. Office of Dietary Supplements. Dietary Supplement Fact Sheet. Zinc.

Neiman, D. 2003. Exercise testing and prescription. McGraw Hill.

Orenstein, B. 2011. An anti-anxiety diet. Everyday Health. http://www.everydayhealth.com/anxiety-pictures/anxiety-foods-that-help-foods-that-hurt-0118.aspx#/slide-9

Orenstein, BW. 2012. Eat a healthy diet to feel better. Everyday Health. http://www.everydayhealth.com/depression-pictures/feel-better-foods.aspx#/slide-10

Pander, C. Epsom salt bath treatments. Discovery fit & health. http://health.howstuffworks.com/skin-care/problems/treating/epsom-salt-baths.htm

Patz, A. Happy Meals: 19 foods for every mood. Redbook. http://www.redbookmag.com/health-wellness/advice/good-mood-foods

Sanchez-Villegas, A; et al. 2012. Fast-food and commercial baked goods consumption and the risk of depression. Public Health Nutrition; 15(3):424-32.

SELF. Health calculators. Burn Calories. http://www.self.com/calculatorsprograms/calculators/

SELF. 5 Foods that fight bloat. www.self.com/flat-abs-guide/foods-that-fight-bloat-slideshow#slide=1

SHAPE. What to eat before a date. http://www.shape.com/healthy-eating/diet-tips/what-eat-date

Singer, N. 2011. Your Recycled Resolutions Are a Boon for Business. The New York Times. http://www.nytimes.com/2012/01/01/business/new-years-resolutions-recycled-are-a-boon-for-business.html?pagewanted=all

Sklar, HL. 2008. Celebrity diet tricks that work (and two that you should avoid). CNN Health. http://articles.cnn.com/2008-12-09/health/healthmag.celebrity.diet.tricks_1_veggies-white-foods-clients/2?_s=PM:HEALTH

Smith, J. 10 Easy Ways to burn an extra 100 calories. Redbook Magazine. http://www.redbookmag.com/health-wellness/advice/burn-extra-calories-easy#slide-5

Stewart, K. 2009. 10 easy portion control tricks. Everyday Health. http://www.everydayhealth.com/diet-nutrition/meal-planning/tips/keep-portion-sizes-in-check.aspx

Teitelbaum, J. 2010. Magnesium for pain relief. Psychology Today. http://www.psychologytoday.com/blog/complementary-medicine/201009/magnesium-pain-relief

Templeton, H. 2011. Happy foods that won't make you gain. Fitbie, MSN. http://fitbie.msn.com/slideshow/happy-foods-won-t-make-you-gain/slide/4

The Economist. 2003. The beauty business: pots of promise. http://www.economist.com/node/1795852

Today books. 2009. The inside scoop on red carpet beauty secrets. http://today.msnbc.msn.com/id/29287821/ns/today-books/t/inside-scoop-red-carpet-beauty-secrets/#.T-O5WVI1WiA

Zelman, K. 2010The truth about kale. WebMD. http://www.webmd.com/food-recipes/features/the-truth-about-kale?page=2

Zeratsky, K. 2010. Stevia: Can it help with weight control? Mayo Clinic. http://www.mayoclinic.com/health/stevia/AN01733

Zerbe, L. 11 Instant Mood-boosting foods. Rodale.com. http://www.rodale.com/brain-food

Chapter 9

Dale, 2012. H. 5 natural scents to energize you. Fitsugar. http://www.fitsugar.com/author/Heather%20Dale

Douglas, E. Natural Homemade Grout & Tile Cleaner. National Geographic, Green Living. http://greenliving.nationalgeographic.com/natural-homemade-grout-tile-cleaner-2469.html

Freeman, D. 2010. Color psychology: how to make your home feel good. WebMD http://women.webmd.com/home-health-and-safety-9/color-psychology

Glink, I. 2010. Best paint colors for every room of your house. CBS News.

Hirsh, A.R. 2008. Effects of odor on perception of age. International Journal of Essential Oil Therapeutics; 2, 131-138.

HGTV. How to create a mood with color. http://www.hgtv.com/decorating/create-a-mood-with-color-9-ways/pictures/index.html

Keys, L. Clean The Inside Of Your Car—Fast. Good Housekeeping. http://www.goodhousekeeping.com/home/cleaning-organizing/hell-on-wheels-jun07

Martocq, V. 2011. 10 decorating ideas to make your house a happy home. Chatelaine. http://www.chatelaine.com/en/article/24038--10-decorating-ideas-to-make-your-house-a-happy-home

Mehta, R, Zhu, RJ. 2009. Blue or Red? Exploring the effect of color on cognitive task performances. Science; 323(5918):1226-9.

Reader's Digest. 6 Secret Laundry Ingredients. http://www.rd.com/advice/6-secret-laundry-ingredients/?v=print

Roto-Rooter. Kitchen Tips and Maintenance. http://www.rotorooter.com/plumbing-basics/plumbing-in-your-home/kitchen-tips-and-maintenance/

Chapter 10

Brufau, G.; et al. 2006. Nuts: source of energy and macronutrients. British Journal of Nutrition; (96):S24–S28

Eating Smart—Kiwi Capers. Cancer Resource Center. http://www.cancerresourcecenter.com/articles/article35.html

Homemade Energy Bars. Tastebook. http://www.tastebook.com/recipes/2221140-Homemade-Energy-Bars?full_recipe=true

Potter, A. 2008. 10 Fresh Ways to Boost Your Energy Now. CNN. http://articles.cnn.com/2008-04-09/health/healthmag.energy_1_protein-blue-light-mariana-figueiro/3?_s=PM:HEALTH

Reader's Digest. Quick ways to boost your energy. http://www.rd.com/health/quick-ways-to-boost-your-energy/

Ahmed, SM; Lemkau, JP; and Hershberger, PJ. 2011. Psychosocial influences on health. Textbook of Family Medicine.

Brown, D; Oh, R. 2003. Vitamin B12 Deficiency. American Academy of Family Physicians; 67(5):979-986.

Brown, R; et al. 2009. How to Use Herbs, Nutrients, and Yoga in Mental Health Care.

Evans, M. 2003. Yoga, Tai Chi Massage, Therapies & Healing Remedies.

Exercise for Stress and Anxiety. Anxiety and Depression Association of America. http://www.adaa.org/living-with-anxiety/managing-anxiety/exercise-stress-and-anxiety

Lakhan, S; Vieira, K. 2010. Nutritional and Herbal Supplements for Anxiety and Anxiety-Related Disorders: Systematic Review. Nutrition Journal.

Larzelere, MM; Jones, GN. 2008. Stress and health. Primary Care; 35:839-856.

Cernya, A, Schmid, K. 1999. Tolerability and efficacy of valerian/lemon balm in healthy volunteers. Fitoterapia; 70(3): 221-28.

Evert, A. 2011. Magnesium in Diet. MedlinePlus Medical Encyclopedia. http://www.nlm.nih.gov/medlineplus/ency/article/002423.htm

Heaney, RP; and Weaver CM. 1990. Calcium absorption from kale. American Society for Clinical Nutrition; 51(4): 656-67.

Reiter, R. Cherry Nutrition Report. Cherry Marketing Institute. http://www.choosecherries.com/Uploads/Documents/8589194263810869558.pdf

Saslow, R. 2011. Can Relaxation Drinks Put You to Sleep? The Washington Post. http://www.washingtonpost.com/wp-dyn/content/article/2011/02/14/AR2011021405988.html

Vorvick, L. 2010. Tryptophan. Medline Plus. http://www.nlm.nih.gov/medlineplus/ency/article/002332.htm

Wright, B. Foods To Help You Sleep. EatingWell Magazine. http://www.eatingwell.com/nutrition_health/nutrition_news_information/9_foods_to_help_you_sleep

Zerbe, L. Eat, Drink, and Be Sleepy! 5 Natural Sleep Aids. MSNBC. http://health.msn.com/health-topics/sleep-disorders/eat-drink-and-be-sleepy-5-natural-sleep-aids

Soman, M. 25 ways to sleep better tonight. Good Housekeeping. http://www.goodhousekeeping.com/health/wellness/sleep-better-tonight

Glickman, A. Time Management. Center for Learning and Teaching, Stanford University. http://www.stanford.edu/dept/CTL/Student/studyskills/time_manage.pdf

Chapter 11

Al Aboud, K; and Khachemoune, A. 2009. Vaseline: a historical perspective. Dermatology Nursing; 21(3):143-4.

Broida, R. 2010. 8 ways to hack bad breath. CBS. http://www.cbsnews.com/8301-505143_162-28646423/8-ways-to-hack-bad-breath/

Discovery. 2005. Myth: can vodka cure bad breath? http://dsc.discovery.com/fansites/mythbusters/db/food/can-vodka-cure-bad-breath.html

Erlich, S. 2012. Licorice. University of Maryland Medical Center. http://www.umm.edu/altmed/articles/licorice-000262.htm

Erlich, S. 2011. Peppermint. University of Maryland Medical Center. http://www.umm.edu/altmed/articles/peppermint-000269.htm

Good, B. 2010. The sex for life diet. Men's Health. http://www.menshealth.com/mhlists/foods_for_sex/Celery.php

Gottlieb, B. 2008. Alternative cures: more than 1,000 of the most effective natural home remedies.

Health Magazine. 2007. Alcohol spa treatments: beer pedicure. http://www.health.com/health/article/0,,20410677,00.html

Kloss, J. 2004.Back to Eden: The classic guide to herbal medicine, natural foods, and home remedies since 1939.

Kiefer, D. 2010. Aloe vera. WebMD. http://www.webmd.com/vitamins-and-supplements/lifestyle-guide-11/supplement-guide-aloe-vera

Mayo Clinic. 2012. Lifestyle and home remedies: ingrown hair. http://www.mayoclinic.com/health/ingrown-hair/DS01167/DSECTION=lifestyle-and-home-remedies

Mayo Clinic. 2011. Lifestyle and home remedies: nail fungus. http://www.mayoclinic.com/health/nail-fungus/DS00084/DSECTION=lifestyle-and-home-remedies

Mayo Clinic. 2010. Moisturizers: Options for softer skin. http://www.mayoclinic.com/health/moisturizers/SN0004

MSN Living. 50 best grooming tips and products for men. http://living.msn.com/style-beauty/well-groomed-male/article?cp-documentid=30943614

MSN Health. 8 home remedies for bad breath. http://health.msn.com/health-topics/oral-care/slideshow.aspx?cp-documentid=100233946&imageindex=1

FC&A Medical Publishing. 2008. Old-fashioned Cures and Proven Home Remedies. Peachtree City, GA: FC&A Medical Publishing.

Prevention Magazine. 2011. Prevention's quick fix: The 5 best home remedies for snoring. http://shine.yahoo.com/work-money/preventions-quick-fix-the-5-best-home-remedies-for-snoring-2469935.html

Surjushe, A; et al. 2008. Aloe vera: A short review. Indian Journal of Dermatology; 53(4):163-6.

The Nail Bar @11th. Spa Menu. http://www.nailbar11th.com/Services.html

Women's Health Magazine. 2010. Love bites. http://www.womenshealthmag.com/sex-and-relationships/foods-that-will-boost-your-sex-drive?page=1

Chapter 12

Brookhart-Schervish, L. 2012. Healthy Snacks Kids (and Moms) Love. Parents. http://www.parents.com/recipes/cooking/kid-friendly-food/healthy-snacks-kids-love/

Danish, E. 2012. Calming Tips for Hyperactive Children. Health Guidance. http://www.healthguidance.org/entry/15022/1/Calming-Tips-for-Hyperactive-Children.html

Lowe's Companies, Inc. 2012. Build and Grow: Free Kids Clinics. http://www.lowesbuildandgrow.com/pages/default.aspx

Michaels Stores, Inc. 2012. Creative Classes. http://www.michaels.com/Exciting-Classes/classes,default,pg.html

The Home Depot U.S.A Inc. 2012. Free Kids Workshops to Learn, Create & Craft at The Home Depot. http://www.homedepot.com/webapp/catalog/servlet/ContentView?pn=HT_WS_KidsWorkshops

Weeden, Colleen. 2012. Fun Finger Foods. Parents. http://www.parents.com/toddlers-preschoolers/feeding/recipes/fun-finger-foods/#page=1

Chapter 13

American Society for Prevention of Cruelty to Animals. Coprophagia. Virtual Pet Behaviorist. http://www.aspcabehavior.org/articles/31/Coprophagia-Eating-Feces.aspx

Arizona Humane Society. 2007. Pet Training: Redirecting your cat's undesirable behavior. http://www.azhumane.org/PDFs/behavior/cats/redirectingbehavior.pdf

Barr, T. 2010. Removing pet Stains and Odors for Dummies. Hoboken, NJ: John Wiley & Sons.

Bozzuto, D. 2001. Antimicrobial Herbs. Jacksonville Medicine. http://dcmsonline.org/jax-medicine/2001journals/Feb2001/herbs.htm

Brunette, D. 1996. Effects of baking soda containing dentifrices on oral malodor. Compendium of Continuing Education in Dentistry; 17(19): S22-23.

Gage, M. Keeping Your Dog Warm and Safe in Your Garage. Pawsitive Experience Dog Training and Behavior Specialist. http://www.pawsitiveexperience.com/Pawsitive_Experience/Training_Tips_files/Keeping Your Dog Warm and Safe in Your Garage.pdf

Gardner, A. 2012. The best and worst foods for digestion. Fox News. http://www.foxnews.com/health/2012/02/06/best-and-worst-foods-for-digestion/

Green, J. 2011. Joey Green's Amazing Pet Cures. New York: Rodale Books.

The American Society for the Prevention of Cruelty to Animals. 2012. Begging at the Table. http://www.aspcabehavior.org/articles/182/Begging-at-the-Table.aspx

The American Society for the Prevention of Cruelty to Animals. 2012. Desensitization and Counterconditioning. http://www.aspcabehavior.org/articles/14/Desensitization-and-Counterconditioning.aspx

The Humane Society of the United States. 2011. Barking: How to Get Your Dog to Quiet Down. http://www.humanesociety.org/animals/dogs/tips/how_to_stop_barking.html

The Humane Society of the United States. 2012. Housetraining Puppies. http://www.humanesociety.org/animals/dogs/tips/housetraining_puppies.html

The Humane Society of the United States. 2010. Teaching Dogs the "Come" Command. http://www.humanesociety.org/animals/dogs/tips/teaching_come_command.html

Yu, A. 1994. Shampoo Therapy in Dogs and Cats. Pedigree Breeder. http://putthepentothepaper.wordpress.com/2008/02/03/shampoo-therapy-in-dogs-and-cats-by-anthony-a-yu-bsc-dvm/